THE STRUCTURE OF
BEOWULF

THE STRUCTURE OF
BEOWULF

BY

KENNETH SISAM

OXFORD
AT THE CLARENDON PRESS
1965

Oxford University Press, Amen House, London E.C.4

GLASGOW NEW YORK TORONTO MELBOURNE WELLINGTON
BOMBAY CALCUTTA MADRAS KARACHI LAHORE DACCA
CAPE TOWN SALISBURY NAIROBI IBADAN ACCRA
KUALA LUMPUR HONG KONG

829.3
Z S S

PRINTED IN GREAT BRITAIN
AT THE UNIVERSITY PRESS, OXFORD
BY VIVIAN RIDLER
PRINTER TO THE UNIVERSITY

CONTENTS

I

INTRODUCTORY

IN a place far from libraries, I have often read the
text of *Beowulf* for pleasure, partly, no doubt, the
pleasure of reminiscence. Re-reading has brought a
fresh interest in some structural problems, on which there
are wide differences of opinion between scholars, especially between scholars of different periods. Not much
can be established with even a moderate degree of probability, and generally we must be content with exploratory views and impressions. There is no one key to the
appreciation of *Beowulf*. But it may be useful to choose
a line of approach, and follow it through even when it
leads to some conflict with predominant opinion.

I start from the position that, though it contains
historical, elegiac, gnomic, and didactic elements,
Beowulf is an heroic narrative poem, composed to
entertain an audience of Anglo-Saxons. So I propose to
discuss selected topics from the point of view of story-
telling for such an audience. To do so requires repetition
of things that have been said already, and mention of
some that are commonly passed over as obvious.[1]

---

[1] References are mostly to the text. References to modern criticism
are given only for special reasons and seldom go beyond the best-known
surveys: the current editions; R. W. Chambers, *Beowulf, an Introduction*
etc., 1921, 3rd edn. supplemented by C. L. Wrenn 1959; H. M. Chadwick, *The Heroic Age*, 1926; W. W. Lawrence, *Beowulf and Epic Tradition*,

I deal with the structure of the poem as it stands in MS. Vitellius A xv, copied round about the year 1000, assuming that its text represents approximately the form given to the story by one man—original poet, or poet-editor, or accomplished reciter able to adapt and vary existing stories in verse. This leaves open the questions whether all three main adventures had been brought together in an earlier stage, and whether practically all the lines were versified by one poet. In what follows, 'the poet' is used to mean the shaper of the text that survives.

We should understand the construction of *Beowulf* better if we knew why it was made so long. Before the twelfth century no secular poem approaching its scale is recorded from the vernaculars of Western Europe. It is longer than the longest poems in other kinds that survive from early Anglo-Saxon times—Aldhelm's *de Virginitate* in Latin and the Old English *Genesis* with its interpolation. But Aldhelm was abridging his prose treatise on the same subject, and *Genesis* is crowded with Biblical narrative. In *Beowulf* many ways of dilating the matter are used: digressions, episodes, speeches, description. By these means the fight with Grendel is made into a fairly long story. And the plot is extended by a primitive method: two more adventures of the hero,

Harvard, 1928; J. Hoops, *Beowulfstudien*, and *Kommentar*, Heidelberg, 1932; Miss D. Whitelock, *The Audience of 'Beowulf'*, 1951; A. G. Brodeur, *The Art of 'Beowulf'*, Berkeley, 1959; H. M. and N. K. Chadwick, *The Growth of Literature*, 1932–40. A short article by J. R. Hulbert, 'The Genesis of *Beowulf*: a caveat' (*P.M.L.A.* xvi, 1951), pp. 1168 ff., is valuable for its caution.

the fights with Grendel's Mother and with the Dragon, are recounted in the same leisurely manner.

At one time leading critics like Müllenhoff[1] explained the form and length of the poem by postulating a number of interpolators who worked over a more shapely, compact, and consistent synthesis of short lays. Recently Heusler[2] has given his authority to the view that *Beowulf* is the work of an ecclesiastic who emulated the epic breadth of Virgil. I prefer to think, with Chadwick,[3] that long secular poems were a native development, to be expected when story-telling was the principal entertainment in the northern winter, and when professional minstrels (*scopas*) had the training necessary to compose or recite an heroic poem that could entertain an audience for hours, even for days. There would be times when a continuous, slow-moving story would please better than the less restful succession of short pieces; and the length of *Beowulf* was well within the capacity of a memory accustomed to work without books.[4]

---

[1] *Beovulf*, Berlin, 1889.

[2] *Die altgermanische Dichtung*, 2nd edn., Potsdam, 1943, p. 192.

[3] *The Heroic Age*, pp. 73 ff.

[4] For the great lengths that may be attained without writing, see C. M. Bowra, *Heroic Poetry*, 1952, pp. 351 ff. Composition without writing is not necessarily the same as improvisation. Improvisation of a comparatively short eulogy of Beowulf is implied in lines 871–4, though there was some time in which to prepare it. But an unlettered poet could work in another way. He could prepare parts of a longer poem on solitary walks or resting in the dark, memorize them, and later link them together. The first recitations would serve as rehearsals, enabling him to make improvements. It is hard to believe that poems like the *Iliad* and *Odyssey* were, in the main, versified by a poet as he recited them. *Beowulf*, with more lapses and more use of devices that help an improviser, has many of the marks of premeditated art.

At the rate of delivery which the dignified style suggests, its 3,182 lines might occupy four hours without pause, so that there would be many occasions when it could not be recited complete at one session. If, as I suppose, *Beowulf* had a life outside books[1]—if it was sometimes recited from memory—it could be adapted to a shorter time by reducing speeches or omitting episodes and digressions. The extant form suggests a serial in three instalments.[2] The fight against Grendel (1–1250) and the fight against the Dragon (2200–3182) fit this suggestion well. The intervening part begins aptly with a recapitulation. Then the encounter with Grendel's Mother and the consequent celebrations are described in some 600 of the best lines in the poem. But they are followed (1888–2199) by Beowulf's return home, with a long recapitulation of his experiences in Denmark, and by scenes at Hygelac's court which cannot be fresh coming so closely after the similar scenes at

[1] See Note A on 'Transmission' at p. 67 below.

[2] See Professor Whitelock's remarks in *The Audience of 'Beowulf'*, p. 20. In *Beowulf* there are no certain forward references from one main adventure to another. The attack by Grendel's Mother comes as a surprise though her existence was known (1345 ff.); and when Hrothgar warns Beowulf of the many ways by which death may come to him (1762 ff.) he mentions nothing like death from a dragon's fangs. It has been said that the reference to Sigemund's dragon-fight (884 ff.) would bring the final adventure to the minds of listeners: so Professor Bonjour writes of 'the audience . . . knowing as they do that Beowulf in his turn was to achieve "dōm unlytel" by killing the Dragon . . .' (*The Digressions in 'Beowulf'*, 1950, p. 47). This implies that the poet retold a familiar story in which the three main adventures were associated. But that is a doubtful assumption. To remind the audience of Sigemund's more complete success was not the happiest way of praising Beowulf; and if the poem ended without the Dragon Fight, modern critics would not find the reference to Sigemund inept.

Heorot, and are colourless by comparison. 'Beowulf's Return' has troubled critics for other reasons. If it was planned to be the closing part of an instalment which began with line 1251, a weakness in construction must be admitted.[1]

Whether or not delivery in instalments based on the three great fights was contemplated, the plot seems to have been built up to meet the demand for another story about the hero who destroyed Grendel. A child who asks for another story about Jack the Giant-Killer expects more giant-killing. A reader of the *Strand Magazine* in the 1890's would have been disappointed if, say, a successful big-game hunt had appeared as an 'Adventure of Sherlock Holmes'. So another story about the destroyer of Grendel suggested one where his marvellous strength and courage were pitted against monsters with which other brave men could not contend. Once the adventure with Grendel's Mother had been added (and the extant text as well as the analogues gives evidence that this sequel is older than the addition of the Dragon Fight) the pattern was established. So, besides the primitive unity of a single hero, there is a second almost as primitive: the adventures are of the same kind.

Where the pattern is so narrowly restricted there is a risk of monotony, and the poem has not escaped criticism on that ground. But its narrowness accounts for the concentration on a few days in Beowulf's long life. Of the rest very little is told, because there was no

[1] See below, pp. 44 ff.

need to invent it for the purposes of this narrative. And though modern tastes and interests may not be satisfied, we should appreciate such strict economy, which throws into relief the unclassical profusion of other kinds of expansion. The same economy appears in details like the description of Grendel: only his right arm with its steel-like claws is sharply realized, because it is the instrument of his destructive power, the trophy of Beowulf's victory, the object—at least in part—of the surprise attack by Grendel's Mother. The light does not fall on the rest of his giant body.

There is a further limitation. Beowulf fights against monsters that lived in the imagination of Anglo-Saxons: sea-monsters that attacked ships and swimmers; man-eating giants; a fiery dragon. There are none of the exotic monsters that a reader of Latin would meet with occasionally in Virgil, or abundantly in such texts as the *Epistola Alexandri*, the Latin *Wonders of the East*, and the *Liber Monstrorum*, of which the last two seem to be compilations made in England in early Anglo-Saxon times.[1] This limitation to native beliefs gives some assurance that the poem, as we have it, is the complete story and not a selection from a larger cycle of Beowulf's adventures. For there were no more monsters of the kind worth killing. It would be ridiculous to match him against elves or dwarfs; more sea-monsters would make an anti-climax,[2] since they

---

[1] On these texts and their connexion with *Beowulf* see Professor Whitelock, *The Audience of 'Beowulf'*, pp. 46 ff., and K. Sisam, *Studies in the History of Old English Literature*, 1953, pp. 72 ff.

[2] Müllenhoff (*Beowulf*, p. 125) noted the weakness of ll. 1432 ff.,

are at best poor material for an Anglo-Saxon poet, wisely consigned to the Breca episode; and one dragon was enough for a Teutonic hero.

For a storyteller, exhaustion of plot-matter raises the question: What is to become of the hero? To let Beowulf live happily ever afterwards would not be satisfying. To picture him weakened by old age, like Hrothgar, and dying in his bed, would be inglorious for the hero who, above everything else, desired glory (3182). To have him die from a wound that made his victory over the Dragon more wonderful was an obvious solution; and it is improved by representing him as an ideal king for fifty years, yet still the strongest of men. I do not suggest that the poet had only this in mind when he planned the ending, but simple considerations should not be neglected.

The monsters might never have reached above the level of folk-tale. Whether or not the credit is due to our poet, it was a stroke of genius that brought Grendel to Heorot, the hall of early Danish kings, where Hrothgar and Hrothulf presided, and where later they defeated Ingeld. The doors of Heorot opened into the Heroic Age: great kings, queens, and heroes, splendid ceremonies, fine speeches, famous stories, harp-playing,

---

where the hero shoots a sea-creature with an arrow before plunging into the mere, and ascribed them to an interpolator. No doubt the incident was intended both to add a touch of realism and to focus attention on Beowulf; but it is out of character for him to do what any of the men present might have done; and in his Dragon Fight, where they might have been useful, he does not use missile weapons—arrows or spear.

all were in place there. It was the ideal setting for a
discursive heroic poem; and so long as the scene is laid
in a royal hall, whether Hrothgar's or Hygelac's, the
poet has no great difficulty of construction. Outside the
hall his machinery is often clumsy.

A great man's hall was particularly suited for the
display of noble conduct which contributes so much to
the dignity of *Beowulf*. We are shown the best side of
the life of heroes as it was imagined in Anglo-Saxon
England. The picture is curiously selective: for example,
the food they ate at their feasts and the clothes they wore
are nowhere mentioned. More significant is the omission
of everything ordinary. No usual work is referred to;
there are no common people—women who spin, weave,
or launder; husbandmen, herdsmen, or fishermen.
A runaway slave chances to find the Dragon's treasure,
but he hardly counts among men. So the subject-
matter, as well as the tone and style of *Beowulf*, has led
many critics to believe that the poem was composed
for recitation at the court of a king or noble. That other
audiences could enjoy it is not a reason for doubting
this primary purpose.

What kind of audience would a poet find there?
Clearly not the men of elegant taste, trained to criticize
literary form and expression, who heard Virgil read the
Aeneid at the court of Augustus. Nor was it like the
audience for whom Chaucer wrote when the English
court was at a peak of luxury and variety in entertainment, with tournaments, pageants, dancing, gay
music, and a wealth of literary kinds that would have

amazed an Anglo-Saxon, especially the literature of love, and tales and satires made to amuse. The taste of any Anglo-Saxon court was unsophisticated in comparison. We may suppose that the listeners would be the kind of people who appear in Heorot: the king, his family, counsellors and officials such as Unferth, Æschere, and Wulfgar; perhaps distinguished visitors or hostages. In Christian times the Church would almost certainly be represented, though not by monks like Cuthbert and Bede or hermits like Guthlac. But the main audience would be the king's bodyguard, who shared his hearth and table (*heorðgeneatas, beodgeneatas*) and in battle formed the core of his army. These men were not chosen mainly for intellectual qualities. They should not be thought of as learned in legendary history or theology, and quick to interpret any difficulty of expression or allusion.[1] Bold rather than delicate effects would suit them best.

[1] The knowledge of heroic legend to be expected from the audience should not be overrated. Some knew more than others. The essentials of some stories, such as those of Ingeld and Finnsburh, would be widely known. In a particular hall the repertory of its recognized *scop* would be a main factor. But enjoyment of poetry does not require the understanding of every allusion, and that degree of perfection is unlikely in a mixed audience. Elsewhere ('Anglo-Saxon Royal Genealogies', *Proc. Brit. Acad.* xxxix, 1953, pp. 345 ff.) I have noted some examples of vagueness, discrepancy, or error in what is recorded of legendary heroes by writers who had time to think.

It is unlikely too that the ordinary listener gave the close attention to the meaning of single words and phrases that is required from a modern commentator or glossary-maker. An examination of the words that are known only from *Beowulf* shows that most of them are transparent compounds or derivatives. The meaning of others can be gathered because of the repetitive character of Anglo-Saxon verse: in 223 f. *þa wæs sund liden | eoletes æt ende*, the sense—that Beowulf had reached the

A good poet will not be limited by the power of appreciation in his immediate audience; but to be successful in the conditions I am assuming, he should not neglect a main part of them. He could, of course, expect fine language,[1] the rhythm of the verse, the reciter's arts, the pleasure of being in good company, to carry listeners untroubled over some places that they did not understand very well or did not find very interesting. But much more was needed to make a long poem entertaining to an audience who were assembled primarily because they were a great man's retainers and his hall was the centre of their fellowship. In fact there is little in *Beowulf* that would not hold the interest of the *heorðwerod*. It would be tedious to work through the poem to establish the point; so I notice some major elements in the content where a modern reader's appreciation is inevitably less than theirs.

Three superhuman creatures would be good measure in any tale of marvellous adventures. But we do not believe in these particular monsters, and are inclined to treat the main plot as childish. For an Anglo-Saxon audience, gathered in a hall as night came on, with

Danish shore—is clear, whether *eolet* means 'sea' or 'voyage' or the like. The context gives a broad indication of the meaning of the much discussed *ealuscerwen* (769), and even those who knew it from other sources may not have known how the meaning arose: many who understand 'a (pretty) kettle of fish' do not inquire why the phrase bears that sense. A competent modern reader probably follows the literal meaning more closely and exactly than most Anglo-Saxons did.

[1] J. H. de Largy, 'The Gaelic Story-Teller' (*Proc. Brit. Acad.* xxxi, 1945), p. 207, records the praise an old story-teller gave to those he had heard in his youth: 'they had such fine hard Irish you would not understand a word from them'.

the dark creeping into corners beyond the firelight, these monsters were real terrors. Even as they listened, a giant from the hills and fens might be prowling outside the doors, a dragon might be leaving his trail in the sky or setting sparks to the thatch.

Again, the treasure story does not excite modern academically trained minds. Yet it cannot be explained away as the vestige of an older story; for, apart from the prominence given to it throughout the third adventure, it is uppermost in Beowulf's thoughts at critical moments. Before he challenges the Dragon he says: 'Now shall the sword's edge, hand and keen blade, do battle for the treasure' (2508 f.); and again: 'I shall win the gold by valour, or the fight will be my death' (2535–7). As he lies dying his great wish is to see some of it with his own eyes (2743 ff.); in his last speech he thanks God for letting him win such a hoard for his people at the price of his life (2794–2800). The poet himself says Beowulf paid for the great and splendid treasure with his life (2842 f.), and is echoed by the authoritative voice of the Messenger (3011 f.). These facts are troublesome to critics who think of Beowulf primarily as one who sacrifices himself to defend his country,[1] or as the type of mankind battling against a

---

[1] At 2335 f. we are told that Beowulf planned vengeance or punishment for the destruction the Dragon had done. But this is not enough to justify Klaeber's comment in his note to the place: 'From the standpoint of the poem, the defense of the country and desire of revenge is the hero's primary motive.' Defence of his country was the obvious duty of a king, and the poet makes very little of it as a motive for fighting the Dragon. But his ideal hero always fights after provocation.

hostile world. But the poet accepted him as a character from the Heroic Age, in which the lure of booty, of wealth to be won by daring, was very strong.[1] And his audience were held by a theme which, after centuries of exploitation, still thrills simple minds. They wanted to know how the treasure was assembled, why and where it was hidden, by what chance it was discovered, how hardly it was won, how great and rich it proved to be, what became of it; and on all these points curiosity is satisfied, even to such particulars as the seven men who helped Wiglaf to bring it out into the daylight and the wagon or wagons that carried it to Hronesness.

Then again there is a great deal of fighting in *Beowulf*—straightforward hand-to-hand fighting without tricks and (except for the sword with which Grendel's Mother is dispatched) without magical aids;[2] and there are many admiring references to arms and armour. The fine arms and armour which Anglo-Saxons dreamed of possessing are now the concern of archaeologists; and though its causes, consequences, or setting may interest a modern reader, he is more inclined to pass over the detailed fighting with apathy

[1] In their general characterization of an heroic age, the Chadwicks note that 'the thought of booty is never to be ignored' (*The Growth of Literature*, iii, 1940, pp. 731 f.). There is a crude example in the account of Beowulf's escape, after Hygelac's defeat at the mouth of the Rhine, by swimming to Sweden: he carried with him not Hygelac's body or some fellow survivor of the disaster, but the 'war gear' stripped from thirty of the enemy (2361 f.). Nothing in the plot requires this marvel; and on the view that the text as we have it is the work of one man, such details are evidence of his way of thinking.

[2] Contrast the Dragon Fight in *Beowulf* with the account of Sigurd's dragon-killing in *Volsunga Saga*.

or even distaste than to enjoy it. But the poet took
pains to make the three fights against monsters the high
points of his story: each sets the hero a new tactical
problem, and in each the action is well imagined,
varied, and realistic. He could be sure that the audience
we have assumed would appreciate them, for war was
endemic in early England, and war was the business of
the *heorðwerod*. Perhaps that explains the long account
of Ongentheow's end about lines 2923–98, which
reads almost like a caricature of the practice of digres-
sion. We are not told how the Geatish king Hæðcyn
(2481 ff., 2924 f.) died in battle, and only the general
circumstances of Hygelac's death are given. But while
Wiglaf waits beside Beowulf's body; while the Geats
are eager to see their heroes, the dead Dragon, and the
treasure; and even the Messenger himself feels the need
for urgent action (3007), he delays it by a long description of Ongentheow's last battle (a story the Geats
must have known well) with such vivid detail that
something of the spirit of the grim old Swedish king
comes through to us. If the hall-company noticed the
structural fault here, they would probably think it
more than compensated by a passage so much to their
taste.

The high standard of conduct that is set throughout
the poem would also have a direct and salutary appeal
to such a company. Beowulf is a flawless hero who
does what is best unfailingly and unhesitatingly. His
expedition to Heorot provides the occasion for a
fascinating lesson in Anglo-Saxon courtly etiquette,

from the time when he was met by the harbour-warden to his elaborate farewell.[1] The one lapse from fine manners (when Unferth asserts that Breca won the swimming match, and Beowulf crushes him with an answer that is ruder and more inconsequent) is soon made good in the best way by magnanimity on both sides.[2]

Another thread that runs through the poem is the ideal relation of lord and man within the *comitatus*, which lived on, at least in some great households, throughout the Anglo-Saxon period. For Beowulf himself the relation is not quite simple; he is *Hygelaces þegn* and also *Hygelaces mæg*—his sister's son. Close kinsmanship would account for the undivided affection expressed at lines 2149 ff., but hardly for

Herebeald ond Hæðcyn   oððe Hygelac *min*[3] (2434).

Personal devotion to one's lord distinguishes the Teutonic from the later feudal system, in which obligations tend to be limited and legally defined. From his first appearance we are never allowed to forget that Beowulf is Hygelac's man.[4] He is proud to have repaid in battle all the gifts that Hygelac gave him (2490 ff.). Should he die in the fight against Grendel's Mother, the rewards that Hrothgar

---

[1] Lines 229 ff. and 1806–1903.

[2] Lines 1455 ff., 1488 ff., 1660, 1807 ff.

[3] The arrangement of the words is conventional (cf. l. 61), but the choice of the final adjective is significant. Restraint in the expression of feelings, very effective here, is characteristic of Beowulf. By comparison *The Wanderer*, especially lines 41 ff., is sentimental.

[4] See e.g. lines 194, 261, 342 f., 407 f.

has given him are to be sent to Hygelac (1482 ff.). When he returns home safely the choicest of them are presented to Hygelac and his queen (2148 ff.). Hrothgar implores him to help 'by Hygelac's life' (2131 f.) because it is the thing dearest to him; and when Hygelac is overwhelmed in a rearguard action, Beowulf at once avenges him (2501 f.).

In his younger days Beowulf is a pattern for retainers; but it is after he has been king for fifty years and has proved himself an ideal lord[1] that the obligations of a *comes* or *gesiþ* are driven home by an extreme example. Wiglaf would rather be burnt by the Dragon's flames than leave his lord to die alone, and his desperate courage turns the scale. The other ten are not cowards in any ordinary sense: the enemy was superhuman and seemingly invulnerable; they had no iron shields; Beowulf had ordered them to keep out of the fight. Yet their failure to sacrifice themselves for him makes them outcasts everywhere: 'death is better for every man than life with dishonour' (2890 f.). This theme, like the display of courtly manners, would appeal directly to a king or great noble and his household.

These are some aspects in which the poem would seem better, more entertaining, to its Anglo-Saxon audience than to a modern academic reader. But I do not suggest that the interests or sympathies of any of them were so limited. When they listened to *Beowulf* they were at

---

[1] This side of the relationship between lord and men is well studied by Schücking, 'Das Königsideal im *Beowulf*', *Englische Studien*, lxvii, 1932, pp. 1 ff.

leisure, not in action, with time to reflect on the many things that reverse happiness: the death of kinsmen or friends; the coming of old age; the sufferings that war brings, especially to women; the wastefulness of blood feuds, which play so large a part in the story. I mention the elegiac element not because it is neglected (the fashion of our day makes too much of it) but because it appeals to feelings as natural in simple as in cultured men. If the poem is considered as entertainment for a hall-company, diversity of mood is one of its great merits; and in this quality no other Anglo-Saxon poem that has come down to us is comparable. Diversity of subject-matter outside of the main plot is also a feature of *Beowulf*, and it is a fair inference that an experienced teller of long stories chose this way of overcoming the monotony of monster-killing by the hero's expeditious methods. If so, we must bear in mind that striving for variety puts a strain on artistic construction, and that the attainment of variety can make a work entertaining which is not elegant in the co-ordination and proportion of all its parts.

II

SURVEY OF GENERAL
INTERPRETATIONS

SEVERAL influential attempts have been made
to find a theme that runs through *Beowulf* and
brings all its parts into greater coherence.

More than a century ago, Müllenhoff proposed a
mythological interpretation. The monsters represent
the hostile North Sea; Beowulf represents a helpful
divinity who fought off successive assaults of the
sea on the low-lying coasts in the spring (Grendel's
Mother is the deep sea); his peaceful reign corresponds
to the summer calm; by fighting against the Dragon
he repulses the storms of autumn; with winter he dies.[1]
Long thought, outstanding scholarship, and an imagination well above the mechanical went to the making
of this hypothesis; yet now it is generally discredited,
together with most of the nature myths that were once
received so readily.

Fashions in scholarship have their interest. Two
conditions contributed to the vogue of the mythological
school. Its exponents had a choice of large, sometimes
vague conceptions—the seasons; sun and moon; night
and day; sea and land, &c.—with which to operate.

---

[1] *Beovulf*, Berlin, 1889, pp. 1–12, where his views, first published in
1848, are finally summarized.

And there was a disposition among leading scholars, as well as among less informed readers, to accept a certain kind of explanation: over this range of ideas the critical faculty was inactive. Müllenhoff was not uncritical. For more than forty years he worked over *Beowulf* and related texts, probing and questioning. He would have regarded as uncritical many of the assumptions that are now deeply entrenched in *Beowulf* studies. But he took it for granted that there was a myth to be found, and did not press the simple question: Why should these monsters represent the North Sea?

The mythological school went beyond natural phenomena. For stories of human affairs they turned to abstractions, often arranged in pairs that may be called 'comprehensive opposites': love and strife, youth and age, &c. Interpretations based on these abstractions tend to be loose; and if several well-selected pairs of opposites are assembled, they form a net into which almost any serious work that has length and variety can be fitted. Take as an example: 'It is a representation of the ceaseless, universal, never decided battle between opposing forces, between rise and fall, waxing and waning, being and not being.'[1] That is not a recent interpretation of *Beowulf*, but Müllenhoff's explanation of the perpetual battle that ends the Scandinavian legend of Hethinn and Högni.

[1] 'Ein bild des unaufhörlichen, allgemeinen, aber nie entschiedenen kampfes entgegengesetzter mächte, des aufgangs und des niedergangs, des entstehens und vergehens, des seins und nichtseins' (*Z. f. d. A.* xxx, 1886, p. 229). I owe the reference to Chadwick, *The Heroic Age*, p. 136 n.

For later opinions one turns naturally to the editions by Klaeber, whose great services to the subject include a conspectus of its vast literature. In his first edition[1] he describes the poet's work on the story: 'Beowulf rose to the rank of a truly ideal hero, and his contests were viewed in the light of a struggle between the powers of good and of evil, thus assuming a new weight and dignity which made them appear a fit subject for the main narrative theme.' 'Good and evil' are perhaps the most comprehensive pair of opposites. Long before Christian times thinkers found in them a basis for classifying everything that affects mankind. So, while it is true that these conceptions play a considerable part in the poem, and that the poet consciously represents some things as good and others as evil, the contrast is too usual to be distinctive: the struggle between good and evil might be said to be the theme, for example, of detective fiction. Other generalities of the kind, of which one of the aptest is the alternation of joy and sorrow, are open to the same objection. They contain an element of truth, but throw little light on the distinctive qualities of *Beowulf*.

At another place in his first edition Klaeber writes: 'We need not hesitate to recognize features of the Christian Savior in the destroyer of hellish fiends, the warrior brave and gentle, blameless in thought and deed, the king that dies for his people.'[2] The idea is repeated more tentatively in a Supplementary Note to

[1] 1922, pp. cxx f.   [2] p. li.

the third edition.[1] I do not like *lucus a non lucendo*.
That Christ is never mentioned in Beowulf is well
known. Christianity in the strict sense of 'Christ's
teaching' scarcely appears, and there is much that is
irreconcilable with it. Beowulf's best-known saying
is: 'Better that a man should avenge his friend than
mourn much' (1384 f.). He avenges Hygelac by
crushing Dæghrefn in his grip (2501 f.). He delights in
material rewards (2101 ff., 2145 ff.). His last thoughts
are of the earthly treasure he has won, the mound that
will keep his memory alive among men, and his ances-
tors (2794 ff.). Beowulf was the ideal hero of men who
were not Christian moralists.[2]

In 1936 Professor Tolkien delivered his lecture on
Beowulf; the Monsters and the Critics,[3] which brought
fresh ideas and has influenced all later writers on the
poem. Knowing well the detailed problems that occupy
critics, he has withdrawn from them to give a general
view of *Beowulf* as poetry, with a fineness of perception
and elegance of expression that are rare in this field.
The lecture, with its subsidiary notes, requires very
careful reading. It does not lend itself to summary or
dissection. As an account of what the poem means to
Professor Tolkien, or of the way in which he, as a
storyteller, would treat the plot, I have no criticism
of it; and on many issues on which he differs from other
critics I agree. But I dissent on two matters which

[1] 1936, p. cxx f., and in the revised edition of 1950.
[2] See Note B on 'Christianity in *Beowulf*' at p. 72 below.
[3] *Proc. Brit. Acad.* xxii. References are to the separate print.

especially concern the structure of the poem. The one
is his explanation of the architecture of *Beowulf* as an
artistic balance between the first two-thirds (1–2199)
and the last part (2200–3182), analogous to the
balance between the two halves of an Anglo-Saxon
alliterative line; the other, his view that the central
theme is the battle, hopeless in this world, of man
against evil.

The idea that the structure of the poem is parallel
with that of its long line has been criticized as fanciful.[1]
On the metrical side the conception of balance is an
elastic one, as may be seen from the variety of half-lines
that are coupled together. But some objective tests can
be applied: for example, a half-line of three syllables
or one having no alliteration would seem unbalanced
to most ears. No such test can be applied to the balance
between the last part of *Beowulf* and the rest. Still the
parallel throws light on the way in which 'balance' is
used. 'The lines . . . are founded on a balance, an
opposition between two halves of roughly equivalent
phonetic weight, and significant content, which are
more often rhythmically contrasted, than similar.'[2]
In the first place 'balance' comes nearest to a primary
sense 'equipoise'. Then we have the sense 'opposition',
'contrast', which does not imply equivalent weight.
And yet a third, more elusive sense is involved in the
discussion, i.e. 'harmony' of design. That its keyword

---

[1] e.g. in a wide-ranging article by van Meurs, 'Beowulf and Literary
Criticism', *Neophilologus*, xxxix, 1955, pp. 114–30.

[2] *Beowulf*, &c., p. 31.

should have such a range of meaning is a weakness of the interpretation.

The nature of the balance in the poem is stated: 'It is essentially a balance, an opposition of ends and beginnings. In its simplest terms it is a contrasted description of two moments in a great life, rising and setting; an elaboration of the ancient and intensely moving contrast between youth and age, first achievement and final death.'[1] Professor Tolkien avowedly favours the mythological school, and follows the method of interpretation by pairs of opposites, which tend to be vague. It is not clear what beginnings in the earlier part and what ends in the last part are opposed, or why Beowulf's rise to the throne should come in the last part. But time will be saved by concentrating on one of the pairs—youth and age.

In the earlier part of the story a distinction between the ages of Beowulf and Hrothgar is necessary: Hrothgar's greatness could not be maintained if he were fit to fight Grendel. 'Hampered by age, he lamented the loss of his youth, of his strength in battle' (2111 ff., cf. 1885 ff.). Beowulf was confident in his strength (669 ff.). Really the contrast lies in this. Hrothgar's age is emphasized, not Beowulf's youth. 'Young' is applied to him only once, when Hrothgar says he has never heard one so young speak more wisely (1843). In over two thousand lines this and Wealhtheow's use of *hyse* (1217) are the express signs that Beowulf is a very young man. Nor is he

---

[1] Op. cit., p. 29.

represented as untried before he fights Grendel. On the contrary, the poet introduces him as the strongest man alive (196 f.). Hrothgar had heard from across the seas that he had the strength of thirty men (377 ff.). Unferth knew of his swimming match against Breca, a prodigious feat even in his version. At the beginning of his first speech in Heorot Beowulf claims: 'I have undertaken many great enterprises in my youth' (408 f.), and goes on to say that the wisest of the Geats had advised him to make the expedition because they had experience of his powers—how he had punished the race of giants and killed sea-monsters in the dark. When he first appears in the story he is a confident and proved hero.

Within the last part there is a contrast between Beowulf's age and Wiglaf's youth, but the emphasis and purpose are different. For Wiglaf, 'young' is the ·stock epithet.[1] The poet shows that when first achievement is in his mind he can express it: 'That was the first time the young warrior had to fight beside his lord' (2625 ff.). And, after the fight, Wiglaf says that it was 'beyond his powers' (2879). Beowulf is often described as old (*frod, gamol, har, eald, ealdhlaford*), but without elaboration. The one express contrast between his age and his youth is not striking.[2] There

---

[1] At lines 2626, 2674, 2675, 2811, 2860; cf. *unfrod* 2821.

[2] 'I have undertaken many warlike adventures in my youth. Now that I am an old king, I will still seek battle and win fame' (2511 ff.). The first sentence echoes the beginning of his speech when he entered Heorot as a young man: hæbbe ic mærða fela | ongunnen on geogoþe (408 f.).

is no suggestion that age was a disadvantage in his fight with the Dragon—that he would have done better had he been younger. He still trusts to his own unaided strength (2540 ff.). The demonstration that no sword could bear the force of his stroke is reserved for this last fight (2684 ff.). The contest is beyond the power of any other man (2532 ff.).

To put my argument shortly—if the two parts of the poem are to be solidly bound together by the opposition of youth and age, it is not enough that the hero should be young in the one part and old in the other. The change in his age must be shown to change his ability to fight monsters, since these fights make the main plot. Instead, Beowulf is represented from beginning to end as the scourge of monsters, always seeking them out and destroying them by the shortest way.

Professor Tolkien's general interpretation—that the monsters symbolize Evil, and that the unifying theme is 'man at war with the hostile world and his inevitable overthrow in Time'[1]—is an original variant of the 'struggle between good and evil'. Most later writers have approved it, but there have been some criticisms. Mr. T. M. Gang[2] noted that he used 'evil' in a range of meanings so wide that a large freedom of interpretation was assured. On the question of method I would add that it is unsafe to attach deep significance to things in which the poet has no choice. For example, if a

---

[1] Op. cit., p. 18.
[2] *R.E.S.* N.S. iii, 1952, pp. 6 f.

proper name has to be introduced into a metre which it does not fit, abnormality is unavoidable and is not good evidence for the poet's voluntary treatment of that metre. The monsters Beowulf kills are inevitably evil and hostile because a reputation for heroism is not made by killing creatures that are believed to be harmless or beneficent—sheep for instance. So the fact that the monsters are evil does not require or favour the explanation that, in the poet's design, they are symbols of evil.[1]

But perhaps the strongest objection to this general interpretation arises from the number of ideas prominent in it that have to be read into the text. One is that Beowulf was defeated, that 'within Time the monsters would win'.[2] There is no word of his defeat in the poem. Wiglaf says, 'Yet God, the giver of victories, granted him that he, single-handed, avenged himself with steel' (2874 ff.); and, according to the poet, the Dragon Fight was 'his last victory' (2710). On the other hand, all the monsters are utterly defeated. The Dragon, the last and most terrible of them, is

---

[1] In some passages of Scripture and of Christian writings the Devil is represented by a 'dragon'. But our Dragon has no likeness to the dragon of the Apocalypse. Among patristic writers, none had greater authority in the West than St. Augustine of Hippo. With Psalm xc. 13 in mind (*conculcabis leonem et draconem*) he says the Devil is represented by the lion *propter impetus*, by *draco propter insidias*. He is thinking of the traditional wiles of the serpent, not of an Anglo-Saxon fiery dragon who was formidable because of his furious assaults (*impetus*) rather than for his guile. Note also that it is a long leap from the local giants who attacked Heorot, and the Dragon who had his den near Beowulf's home, to the cosmic monsters of later Scandinavian tradition.

[2] Op. cit., p. 22.

killed, robbed of his treasure, and his burnt-out carcass is shoved contemptuously into the sea (3131 ff.).

Another is the limitation of man's inevitable defeat to 'Time'. The contrast between life on earth and after-life, between Time and Eternity, was attractive to a Christian poet, yet it is not discussed in the text.

A third is the idea, often repeated, that the poet represents the courage of the Heroic Age as the courage of despair. It is hard to think of Beowulf as hopeless. He is praised by the poet because he has no fear of death.[1] He never broods on death or on life beyond it. When he surveys his own life on his last day, he has little to regret, much to recall with contentment.

These three ideas seem to be essential to the interpretation, which invites the question: Why should a poet, having a great theme in mind, so conceal or disguise it that it has escaped 'the wisdom of a hepe of lerned men' in modern times? No reason has been given why an Anglo-Saxon audience should be more perceptive.

In a discussion which has been mentioned already,[2] Klaeber noted that the poem has 'a markedly edifying character which requires to be analyzed and explained'; and in a footnote he cites some far-fetched explanations as showing 'how urgently the necessity is felt of finding an additional, ulterior motive of some kind'. The existence of this feeling suggests that, for many modern critics, *Beowulf* in its plain meaning does not come up

---

[1] 'So shall a man do when he aims to win lasting praise in battle—he does not worry about his life' (1534 ff.; cf. 1442).

[2] Above, p. 19, p. cxx of the third edition.

to the ideal standards they have set. Still, that does not compel us to search for some master-key, lost since Anglo-Saxon times. Possibly the standards assumed are inappropriate; certainly Anglo-Saxon taste and appreciation were very different from ours. Such reasons may account for the feeling that something essential to the understanding of the poem has been missed. It is questionable too whether a sense of 'urgent necessity of finding an additional, ulterior motive of some kind' makes for sound criticism, since it has brought writers who know the poem well to such strangely conflicting interpretations.

The uniqueness of *Beowulf* has its disadvantages. In Anglo-Saxon, or elsewhere in early Germanic literature, there is nothing comparable in age, content, and fullness of interest. So university teachers of Anglo-Saxon face a dilemma. Unless they neglect the greatest literary text in this field, they must, year after year, work over ground that has been very intensively worked already. The pressure to find something new is strong, and one of its consequences is a tendency to speculate on the things that are not expressed in *Beowulf*.

The kind of general interpretation that has been favoured in recent years[1] depends on two main assumptions. First, that the author of *Beowulf* was widely read in patristic writers: for this the text supplies no evidence in references or citations. Secondly, that he learned from patristic writers to use allegory; but

---

[1] Note the preponderance of this kind in L. E. Nicholson's *Anthology of Beowulf Criticism*, Notre Dame, U.S.A., 1963.

though they, writing for learned readers, felt it necessary to explain their allegorical interpretations, he felt no need of explanation when composing poetry for an audience who preferred the vernacular. The divergent results that have already been derived from these assumptions should throw doubt on their validity.

III

SOME PROBLEMS

1

THE RETURN FROM THE MERE

Lines 837–927

BEOWULF has torn off Grendel's arm and fastened it above the hall door. On the morning after, many assembled there. Leading men (*folctogan*) on their horses followed Grendel's tracks until they came to the mere, which was stained with his life-blood. They rode back in high spirits, praising Beowulf, or racing their horses where the going was good. A king's thane made verses to celebrate Beowulf's victory, and, as part of them, told everything about Sigemund's marvellous adventures, particularly how he killed a dragon and won its treasure. Next—apparently because there was some old association of Sigemund and Heremod[1]—the story of Heremod was taken up, though it has little relevance:[2] of great

---

[1] Their names occur together in the Elder Edda (*Hyndlo-ljóþ* 7 f.).

[2] The element of contrast is too slight to be effective. Sigemund and Beowulf had great daring, but so had Heremod (902). Heremod soured as he grew older, perhaps he was corrupted by power; but Beowulf had not yet been tested in that way. Later on (1709 ff.) the example of Heremod is aptly used by Hrothgar, and artistry cannot be claimed for the anticipation here.

promise in his youth, he became an avaricious and bloodthirsty tyrant, and was done to death among the Jutes. Beowulf, the poet comments, was a more lovable character to everybody. Then, after racing again (916 f.), the horsemen suddenly fade from the story. They do not report their great news, nor is their return linked in any way with what follows. Instead, there is a note of time (917 f.): *Ða wæs morgenleoht | scofen ond scynded*; a crowd assembled at the hall to see the wonderful sight there; Hrothgar and Wealhtheow with attendants came from their bedchamber; Hrothgar thanked God when he saw Grendel's arm; and the story goes on as if the expedition to the mere had never been.

When dissection was in fashion, this was explained by interpolation.[1] The poem would be more shapely, if less interesting, without the expedition; and the explanation seemed more likely because the way that the horsemen found easy and pleasant was difficult and eerie for the party who set out next morning to find Grendel's Mother. The possibility that the expedition is a later addition cannot be excluded, but there are considerations on the other side. To follow Grendel's tracks was a natural thing to do; it had probably been done before (132), and after the attack by Grendel's Mother her tracks were followed (1390 f., 1402 ff.). He might be found dead on the way, or lurking somewhere, still alive and dangerous. If he had reached a refuge, it was important to know

---

[1] Müllenhoff, *Beovulf*, pp. 119 ff.

exactly where. At sight of the bloodstained mere, an immediate release of high spirits—horse-racing and acclamations of Beowulf—was also natural, and there is no place for it once the ceremonial thanksgiving begins with Hrothgar's appearance.

But an improbability arises from the accepted interpretation. Though the mere was not many miles from Heorot (1361 f.), an expedition which followed Grendel's tracks on the way there, and heard all the adventures of Sigemund, with more besides, on the way back, must take a considerable time. Accordingly *Ða wæs morgenleoht | scofen ond scynded* is rendered 'the morning wore on' (Klaeber), or 'hastened to its close' (Dobbie), or 'was past' (von Schaubert), or 'it was mid-day (?)' (Grein–Köhler). Is it credible that on this great day Hrothgar would stay so late in his bedchamber, instead of coming as early as possible to see the evidence of his deliverance? It will not do to say that he was old and infirm, for after the unexpected attack by Grendel's Mother, he had heard the news and summoned Beowulf at first light (1311).

The explanation is better found in a well-known characteristic of primitive narrative: two things happening at the same time are described one after the other with no technical device to show that they were contemporaneous. Here the setting out of the party who follow Grendel's tracks and Hrothgar's appearance to join the crowd outside the door of Heorot are nearly simultaneous. A poet who knew

Virgil could have used *pars . . . pars . . .*, taking care to keep the first member short. Instead, the poet of *Beowulf* describes the expedition to the mere elaborately, and when he comes to the scene at the hall, is unable to make a smooth connexion. He simply repeats the note of time; for I take *Ða wæs morgenleoht | scofen ond scynded* to be practically a variation of *on morgen* (837), meaning 'it was full daylight' or perhaps 'the sun rushed up'.[1]

Whatever explanation of the extant text is preferred, the impressions of the way to the mere given on this occasion and on the following day (1357 ff., 1408 ff.) are strikingly different. If interpolation is excluded, it must be allowed that the poet used to the limits an artist's privilege of varying or selecting material in order to express a mood.

[1] For the Anglo-Saxons there was something urgent in the coming of morning and evening, or the movements of sun and moon. So in *Genesis A*: Metod æfter *sceaf . . .* æfen ærest . . . *þrang* þystre genip (136–9); þa com ofer foldan *fus* siðian | mære mergen þridda (154 f.).

2

DID he use a structural device—mere juxtaposition of subject-matter—in order to suggest ideas that are not otherwise expressed? Important implications have been seen, for example, in Queen Wealhtheow's appearance after the Finn episode had been recited (1162 ff.), and in the nearby reference to Unferth (1165–8).

Wealhtheow and Hildeburh

Earlier critics took the Finn episode to be simply a report of the heroic lay chosen by Hrothgar's *scop* to entertain the company in Heorot; and that is a tenable explanation. Those who expect more subtlety look for some deeper reason why the Finn story was chosen. The episode begins with the sorrows of Hildeburh who lost her brother, son, and husband in the fighting. When the recitation is finished Wealhtheow comes forward, greets Hrothgar, and declares her confidence that Hrothulf (who is sitting beside him) will treat their sons generously if he survives Hrothgar. It is supposed that the audience of *Beowulf*, knowing that trouble was to come between Hrothulf and Hrothgar's family, perceived a parallel between Hildeburh's losses and those that Wealhtheow would suffer. An examination of this view leads into a tangle of problems, particularly the character of Hrothulf; and that must be the excuse for an accumulation of notes on the evidence, which a reader interested in following the thread of argument will do well to pass over. I take the chief characters in turn—Hildeburh, Hrothgar, Hrothulf, and Wealhtheow.

That Hildeburh should be given a principal part in the Finn episode is not surprising. She was a central figure, with her dearest kin on opposite sides. Her sorrows were like the sorrows of Gudrun in the later Icelandic *Guðrúnarkviða*,[1] with the difference that Hildeburh suffered innocently (1072). I suppose that well-known heroic stories were varied by treating them with special reference to one or other of the principal characters; that there might be, for instance, another treatment in which Finn's part was developed. Certainly our poet, like other Anglo-Saxons, had a taste for pathetic situations, such as that of Hrethel (2435 ff.) or of the last survivor of his people (2233 ff.).

Hrothgar has been king of the Danes for fifty years. On the day when Beowulf's victory over Grendel is celebrated, Hrothulf, son of his younger brother Halga, sits beside him and is clearly the second man among the Danes. Their long association was famous. Yet 1163 ff.

> þær þa godan twegen
> sæton suhtergefæderan;   þa gyt wæs hiera sib ætgædere,
> æghwylc oðrum trywe[2]

seem to imply that a quarrel between them broke it. A good deal of learned romance has grown up around

---

[1] *Corpus Poeticum Boreale*, i, p. 323.
[2] 'To where the good pair sat, nephew and uncle; their harmonious association still endured; each was true to the other.'

the interpretation of *þa gyt*.[1] Really nothing is known. Hrothgar's age is exaggerated for the purposes of the story, and the poem leaves the impression that he will die of old age (1873 ff.). That would agree with one Scandinavian tradition, the *Little Chronicle of the Kings of Lejre*.[2] According to Saxo (*c.* 1200) he was killed by the Swedish conqueror King Hothbrod and avenged by his brother Halga.[3] In yet another story, recorded late, he was killed by Hrethric. There is no tradition (I exclude conjectural interpretations) that Hrothulf was concerned in his death. On the succession of Danish kings at this date, and the circumstances that decided it, the relatively late Scandinavian sources are conflicting and untrustworthy.[4]

Hrothulf, for most recent critics, is a traitor who seized power by murdering Hrethric, probably also

---

[1] See Note C at p. 80 below.

[2] Cited by Chambers, *Introduction*[3], pp. 204 f.

[3] Ed. A. Holder, pp. 52 f.

[4] In one group (including Saxo) Halga succeeds Hrothgar and Hrothulf succeeds his father Halga. Another, headed by the pedigree-list of Danish kings called *Langfeðgatal*, runs (in English equivalents): Ingeld, foster-son of Starkath—his brother Healfdene—his sons Hrothgar and Halga—Hrothulf Halga's son—Ingeld's son Hrethric 'the Niggard of Rings'—his son Froda—his son Healfdene—his son Hrethric 'the Thrower-away of Rings'. Professor Malone's reconstruction is a warning against attempts to make history out of such sources. He proposes to delete Froda and his son Healfdene; to treat Hrethric the Niggard and Hrethric the Lavish as one person in two aspects; to substitute Hrothgar for Ingeld as Hrethric's father. Then Hrothulf is succeeded by the Hrethric of *Beowulf*. But that does not suit the view that Hrothulf murdered Hrothgar and Hrethric and seized the throne. So emend to read 'Hrothulf—Hrethric—Hrothulf', assuming that Hrethric was able to drive out Hrothulf for a time with the help of the Geats. (*P.M.L.A.* xlii (1927), pp. 276 ff.; cf. Chambers, *Introduction*[3], pp. 447 ff.)

murdering Hrothgar who was too old to fight, and
possibly murdering Hrothmund, for Richard III and
the little princes in the Tower have had their influence
on the modern legend. Yet in all sources, early and
late, he is a character to be admired. He appears in the
post-Conquest list of heroes popular among the English
which Imelmann discovered in MS. Vespasian D iv.[1]
Scandinavian traditions agree in making him the
best and most glorious of early Danish kings. In
Beowulf he says and does nothing. Why then was he
introduced? I suppose because his name, like Hrothgar's, was so closely connected with the glory of Heorot
that a great occasion there would lose some of its
brilliance without him. Note how carefully the poet
shields him from competition or reproach. When
Beowulf arrives to fight Grendel, Hrothulf, apparently,
is not in the hall. Unferth has the part of the Danish
champion, and he, not Hrothulf, has to submit to
Beowulf's taunt that, if he were as brave as he claimed,
Grendel would never have made such ravages (590 ff.).
Note also that nothing but praise of Hrothulf is
expressed: he and Hrothgar are 'valiant' (1016);
they are 'that good pair, nephew and uncle' (1163 f.).
Irony[2] will not serve to reverse the plain meaning
here, since Hrothgar is involved. It is a strange way
of presenting Hrothulf to an audience if they knew he
was a traitor to his lord, a murderer of his helpless

[1] Accessible in Chambers, *Introduction*[3], p. 252 n.

[2] That dramatic irony was used in Anglo-Saxon heroic poetry is an
assumption. Where it has been detected, the Anglo-Saxon audience is
supposed to have known something conjectured by a modern critic.

benefactor, a usurper of the throne. As far as I re-
collect, no critic has reconciled the modern interpretation of *þa gyt wæs hiera sib ætgædere* with what is express
in *Beowulf*.

Certainly Saxo, writing about the year 1200 and
following here the lost *Bjarkamál* of perhaps two centuries
earlier, reports that Hrothulf, with a fleet, attacked Røric
(presumably Hrothgar's son Hrethric) and killed him.[1]
Saxo is a late and uncritical collector of legends; but if his
report is to be trusted, this is counted among Hrothulf's
good deeds. Røric is represented as a coward. He is
nicknamed 'the Niggard', and niggardliness too was an
unforgivable sin in a Teutonic prince. Though the story
of a popular hero such as Hrothulf is likely to be biased
in his favour, that consideration does not authorize
critics to use a tradition while reversing its sense.

It may be said that *res ipsa loquitur*, that Hrethric was
the rightful heir to the throne and Hrothulf could
become king only by ingratitude and disloyalty.
Hereditary kingship is accepted in *Beowulf*, but not
the strict rule of primogeniture. The good king
Hrothgar did not make way for his elder brother's son
Heoroward.[2] The Danes may not have expected or
wished Hrothulf to become subordinate to Hrethric.

---

[1] Ed. Holder, pp. 62 f. This need not and probably does not mean
that he killed him with his own hands. Hygelac is called 'slayer of
Ongentheow' in *Beowulf* 1968, but it is made clear later (2961 ff.) that
he was killed by Hygelac's men Eofor and Wulf.

[2] Queen Hygd asked Beowulf to be king because her son Heardred
was too young (2369 ff.). Beowulf's refusal is represented as ideal
conduct; but the storyteller may have had another reason for it. The
tradition of Geatish and Swedish affairs in and soon after Hygelac's reign

The words of Wealhtheow herself are instructive. She asks Hrothgar to leave his kingdom to his kin (*magum*), where *bearnum* or *sunum* would have excluded Hrothulf. She is sure that, if Hrothgar dies first, Hrothulf will 'take good care of the young men (*þa geogoðe*)';[1] and expects him to treat her sons as generously as he himself had been treated. If we are depending on implications (and they are dangerous stuff in a poem so loose in thought and expression), this implies that Hrothulf will govern after Hrothgar's death, possibly as senior ruler in association with Hrethric.

Wealhtheow's part in the scene is that of an ideal queen, devoted to her family, perfect in ceremonial. After Hrothgar has rewarded Beowulf, and his *scop* has recited the Finnsburh story, she comes forward, passes the first cup to her lord as courtesy required, and has good words in turn for Hrothgar, Hrothulf, Beowulf (to whom she gives a queen's gifts), and the rest of the company. A modern reader may feel it to be ominous that nobody answers her; but the explanation is that *Beowulf* has none of the quick exchanges that make dialogue, and speeches in reply would have broken the

was evidently precise in many details, and if Heardred was known to be Hygelac's successor, Beowulf could hardly be made to succeed Hygelac. The offer and its refusal would give him the honour without contradicting tradition.

[1] I take *þa geogoðe* to mean the rising generation of unproved men with whom Hrethric and Hrothmund sit (1190). On them the future of the people depended. So under Hrothgar's rule *seo geoguð* 'grew up to be a mighty band' (66 f.). *Arum healdan* (1182) is used elsewhere of the harbour-warden taking care of Beowulf's ship (296), and of King Finn promising to treat the survivors of Hnaef's company generously during the truce (1099).

thread here. I doubt if any audience, hearing the poem recited, would be ingenious enough to detect a parallel between Hildeburh at the funeral of her son and brother and Wealhtheow at this feast of national rejoicing. If the Finnsburh episode were omitted, nothing Wealhtheow says or does need be altered and there would be no loose ends. She did not lose a brother in a quarrel between her own people (the Helmings) and her husband's. There is no good tradition that her husband was killed in a quarrel among the Danes. The similarity would be remote even if the audience knew a story in which she survived to mourn the killing of her son Hrethric: that is a possibility—it should not be treated as a fact.

Besides, there are signs that a parallel between Wealhtheow and Hildeburh was not in the poet's mind. In the Finnsburh episode the course of events after Hnaef's funeral is indicated, and Hengest's situation is fresher in the minds of the audience when Wealhtheow appears. Again, the episode is followed by: 'The gleeman's song was ended; the sound of merriment rose again, the noise from the benches grew loud; servers poured out wine from splendid vessels. Then Wealhtheow came forward, &c.' The poet could hardly have made clearer the change of subject and the transition from tragedy to rejoicing. As I understand the passage, this mood of rejoicing continues throughout Wealhtheow's speeches. It is contrasted, not with her future, but with the attack by Grendel's Mother: 'they did not know the grim event that was to follow', &c. (1233 ff.).

Unferth

1162 ff.

> þa cwom Wealhþeo forð
> gan under gyldnum beage   þær þa godan twegen
> sæton suhtergefæderan;   þa gyt wæs hiera sib æt-
>   gædere,
> æghwylc oðrum trywe.   Swylce þær Unferþ þyle
> æt fotum sæt frean Scyldinga;   gehwylc hiora his
>   ferhþe treowde,
> þæt he hæfde mod micel,   þeah þe he his magum nære
> arfæst æt ecga gelacum.

Following up the inference that Hrothulf turned traitor, many critics suppose the poet implies here that Unferth also was a traitor, though both Hrothgar and Hrothulf were sure of his great courage.[1] According to Brodeur: 'The fact of Unferth's ultimate treachery cannot be doubted: the poet establishes beyond question his complicity in Hrothulf's treason (ll. 1164[b]–68[a])'.[2] Again no reason is given why the treachery of a character from the distant past should be referred to so cryptically. The Ganelons and Modreds of other medieval poems are called traitors in plain words.

While Hrothulf and Halga clearly belong to other stories, probably well known to a particular hall-company because they were in the repertory of its

---

[1] A notable exception is Professor Bonjour, *The Digressions in 'Beowulf'*, pp. 17 ff.

[3] *The Art of 'Beowulf'*, p. 153. Cf. Chambers, *Introduction*[3], p. 27: 'Unferth is evil'; p. 29: 'That the feud [between Hrothgar and Hrothulf] was due to the machinations of the evil adviser can hardly be doubted by those who have studied the ways of old Germanic heroic story.'

scop, Unferth has all the marks of a character developed
for the story of Beowulf's visit to Heorot. He does
exactly what is required for that story and no more.
His name *Un-frith* means 'strife' and at his first appearance, where he serves to introduce the adventure
with Breca, he picks a quarrel with Beowulf. For the
part he plays he must be eminent: he is Hrothgar's
þyle 'spokesman', with a place of honour at the king's
feet (cf. 500). Beowulf calls him 'far-famed' (*widcuð*
1489). He owns the sword Hrunting that has never
failed in battle, and so provides the incident of its
generous loan and return (1455 ff., 1807 ff.). He must
be an active champion, not an old man like Hrothgar
or Æschere: otherwise Beowulf's taunt that he had
not stopped Grendel's raids would be ineffective.
Another taunt, equally irrelevant to the truth of his
account of the swimming-match with Breca, was no
doubt reckoned more crushing when it was devised:
Unferth had killed his brothers in a quarrel (587). One
is tempted to think that some mitigating circumstances
enabled him to keep Hrothgar's favour and trust; but
probably the poet was more concerned to give Beowulf
a withering retort than to reconcile the crime with
Unferth's position. Other references to Unferth (503–5,
1466) confirm the belief of Hrothgar and Hrothulf
that he was a brave man, short of being a match for
Grendel: that would have spoiled the story. There is
no evidence that he had the part of a traitor or evil
counsellor in a time of strife between Hrothulf and
Hrothgar's family.

Lest I seem to be over-zealous in whitewashing villains, I take a less complicated example of the tendency to read too much trouble into the text. King Heorogar left his battle-gear to Hrothgar, not to his son Heoroweard, 'though he loved him well'; and Hrothgar gave it to Beowulf (2155 ff.). Eminent critics (e.g. Olrik, Chambers, Lawrence, Hoops, von Schaubert) think that Heoroweard was slighted. But Hygelac gave Hrethel's sword to Beowulf, not to his son Heardred (2190 ff.); Hrothgar gave his splendid war-saddle to Beowulf, not to his son Hrethric (1038 ff.); Wealhtheow gave a neck-ornament that rivalled the *Brosinga mene* to Beowulf, not to any of her children (1195 ff.). The inference that it was the custom of good rulers to slight their children in this way should not be preferred to the simple explanation that the poet wanted to emphasize the rarity and pricelessness of the gifts made to Beowulf.

The attitude of ordinary Anglo-Saxons to their heroic age is at issue in these interpretations. The occasion was a feast of rejoicing in the most famous of royal halls. Looking back on it, Beowulf, whose virtues included judgement and foresight, says: 'So King Hrothgar lived the good life' (2144), with no hint of internal trouble brewing. Yet according to one critic or another, Hrothulf was a traitor waiting for a chance to seize the throne by murdering his benefactors; Unferth too was a traitor, trusted by both sides; Wealhtheow, fighting for the interest of her sons, suspected Hrothulf, and even Hrothgar's policy of 'adopting' Beowulf. How did this set of schemers get the reputation of heroes? Reading the text without gloss, I think the poet and his audience felt that the Heroic Age was more glorious than their own.

3

BEOWULF'S RETURN
Lines 1888–2199

THIS part of the poem has had few admirers. In *Beowulfs Rückkehr*[1] Schücking surveyed earlier criticism and argued that the whole passage is the work of a poet-editor who aimed at bridging the gap between two separate stories—Beowulf's adventures at Heorot and the Dragon Fight. Tolkien felt that the poem's 'only serious weakness, or apparent weakness, is the long recapitulation: the report of Beowulf to Hygelac'.[2] My concern here is to see how the 'Return' passage fits into the extant form of the poem.

As a bridge between the first two adventures and the last it is unsuccessful, since lines 2200 ff. would come little less abruptly if they followed line 1887 or line 1904. But no clear break defines the beginning of the passage. The pause before line 1888, which is the starting-point preferred by later scholars such as Schücking and Tolkien, is due to the appreciation of Hrothgar (1885–7) which marks his passing out of the narrative. Beowulf remains and this is his story.

The poet seems unable to contrive an effective stopping-point once Beowulf's work at Heorot is done; and in the narrative, as distinct from the episodes, he follows a course which requires no power of inventive construction. The Danish port-warden had met

---

[1] Halle, 1905.   [2] *Beowulf*, &c., pp. 30 f.

Beowulf on his arrival; he is rewarded on Beowulf's return (1890–1903). The hero boards his ship and the voyage home is as swift and uneventful as before. They sight the cliffs of Geatland as before they had sighted the cliffs of Denmark. This time they are met by the Geatish port-warden. They make their way to Hygelac's hall near by, where Beowulf reports his adventures and presents all the magnificent rewards he has won to Hygelac and Hygd. Then comes an appreciation of Beowulf (2177–89) which looks like the winding-up of this part; and finally, in the manner of an afterthought, a short account of how Hygelac rewarded him.

Every step in the sequence of the narrative is obvious. Nor is the framework 'loaded with ore'. The Geatish court is lifeless: Hygelac and Hygd are little more than names of a good king and his good queen. Yet the dignified expression remains and there is no demonstrable falling-off in the technical quality of the metre. The 'Return' reads like the work of a well-equipped poet who has temporarily lost his inspiration, and drifts when he has not another adventure to tell of.

Beowulf's recapitulation (2000–2162), the longest speech in the poem, has been criticized for its length, for its repetition of what has been told already, and for its variations from the earlier narrative. On the first two counts some defence can be made. He had a great deal to report, and to shorten this speech appreciably would make still more noticeable the thinness of the whole passage under discussion. There is also a question of verisimilitude. In early times, when the sources of news were few, a traveller's story on his return was a rare opportunity. A man so famous as Beowulf, who had gone on a great adventure, would be expected to report what had happened. In the circumstances, repetition was inevitable.

The variations from the early narrative have been taken as evidence of interpolation, or of the use of two parallel versions. Others have explained them as intended to relieve the monotony of repetition, though this purpose would not account for all of them. Consideration should also be given to the conditions of pre-literary composition and oral delivery, for *Beowulf* shows many characteristics of verse that was not composed in writing or intended to be read, among them kinds of variation that seem strange to a careful modern reader.

1. Beowulf told Hrothgar that the wise leaders of his people encouraged him to undertake the fight with Grendel (415 ff., cf. 202 f.). Yet, on his return, Hygelac, whose advice mattered most, says he had urged him again and again not to meddle with the murderous ogre, but to let the Danes fight their own battle (1992 ff.). This illustrates a way of presentation which I have noted elsewhere:[1] the poet exaggerates a mood or argument in order to make a strong impression, and at another place, for the same immediate purpose, says something inconsistent. When Beowulf reached Heorot, he had to convince Hrothgar that he was a match for Grendel, and the unanimous advice of the

[1] Above, p. 32; below, p. 58.

wiser Geats who knew his powers would confirm his claims. To mention Hygelac's fears would have spoiled the effect. When Beowulf comes home safe, Hygelac expresses the joy and relief of the Geats—feelings which are effectively conveyed by emphasizing previous anxiety about the outcome of his adventure.

2. Verisimilitude helps to account for the naming of Hondscio at line 2076. When the poet described the struggle in Heorot, it was enough that Grendel began by seizing and devouring one of Beowulf's men. But for Beowulf, back in Hygelac's hall where his small company were all well known, 'one of my men' would not do. The name must be given, with the explanation that he was sleeping nearest to the hall-door, perhaps the post of honour for a bodyguard.

3. Earlier in the story we are told that Grendel, raiding Heorot, ate fifteen of his victims, and carried off home another fifteen (123, 1582 f.). Now (2085 ff.) it appears that, as a bag for his prey, he used a *glof*—a giant's fingerless glove, cunningly made by black magic from snakes' skins. The 'glove' involves no inconsistency. It is an example of a technique noticeable elsewhere in *Beowulf*: from a background that has been kept completely dark the poet brings into the light some realistic detail, not at the first opportunity, but when he wants it to embellish the story. In the same way 'brave Heoroweard', Hrothgar's nephew, appears unexpectedly at line 2161, with the history of a standard, helmet, corslet, and sword which had been simply listed at lines 1020-3.

4. Freawaru, Hrothgar's daughter, is not mentioned on any of the occasions when Beowulf is entertained in Heorot. Her mother Wealhtheow does all the duties of hostess. In the account of his reception Beowulf mentions the queen first, but adds (2020 ff.) that Freawaru was also serving the company; that Hrothgar hoped to secure peace by her betrothal to Ingeld, leader of the Heathobards; and that, in his opinion, the marriage would lead to a tragic quarrel. Thus he introduces the Ingeld episode in the form of a prediction.

Though Freawaru might have been noticed in the earlier narrative, there is no point at which it was necessary or convenient. At the first meeting in Heorot attention is concentrated on the principals—Beowulf, Hrothgar, Unferth (to introduce the Breca story), and Wealhtheow. There is plenty of subject-matter; and even if there were room, Beowulf could not express his misgivings while he was the guest of the Danish court. It was different when he reported to Hygelac, for whom the alliances and quarrels of his neighbours the Danes had a special interest.[1] A first-hand opinion from his right-hand man that there would be war with the Heathobards was great news; and Beowulf's prediction, which

---

[1] Some recent critics, notably Brodeur in *The Art of Beowulf*, pp. 81 ff., attach great significance to a 'treaty' made in Beowulf's farewell speech (1826 ff.) which assured Hrothgar of military support from the Geats. If the poet took this seriously, it would be extraordinary that Beowulf omits to mention it in his report to Hygelac. His silence suggests that he said all the things that were best for the occasion in his farewell speech to Hrothgar. It was ideal conduct, not practical politics.

the audience knew to be accurate,[1] was intended to show his wisdom and foresight. Any long break in the narrative has formal disadvantages; but this episode seems to me to be skilfully introduced at the best place.

5. No such aptness can be claimed for the so-called 'Thryth' episode. In the transmitted text, with editorial patching, it falls so ineptly that Sir William Craigie thought it was a scrap from the manuscript of another poem which had got into the scribe's pattern copy by some mischance.[2] It is the story of an arrogant princess who had been criminally merciless to suitors until the Continental Offa (Offa I) married her, when she became an excellent queen.[3] I have maintained elsewhere[4] that *modþryðo*, with which it begins, is the accusative of an abstract noun, as in so many phrases with *wæg*, e.g. *Genesis* 2238 *higeþryðe wæg*; and that the episode is mutilated at the beginning, where one would expect to find the names of the princess, her father, and her people.

Even so it is a crude excrescence. With Hygelac's hall in view and great news for his king, Beowulf is held back on the beach where he landed while the poet tells this story. To say that it is relevant because, before she was married, the cruel princess was unlike Hygd, does not justify the construction: almost anything could

---

[1] The popularity of the Ingeld story, even among some of the higher clergy, is established by Alcuin's letter of 797 to the bishop of Lindisfarne, from which *Quid Hinieldus cum Christo?* is often quoted (*Mon. Germ. Hist.*, *Epist. Karol. Aevi*, ii, pp. 181 ff.). There is also the evidence of *Widsith* 45–49.   [2] *Philologica*, ii, 1923–4, pp. 16 ff.
[3] See Note D at p. 83.   [4] *Studies*, &c., p. 41 n.

be dragged in on the ground of more or less likeness or unlikeness. The old suggestion that this passage points to contact with the court of the Mercian Offa (d. 796) is attractive because it ends with the names of three members of the Mercian royal house. But perhaps it is a sufficient explanation that the poet aimed at entertainment. If the extraneous stories he wanted to use fitted neatly into the narrative, so much the better; if not, they were still good entertainment. 'Beowulf's Return' would be thinner and more monotonous without the two episodes. As a whole, the 'Return' appears to be an extension of the two older stories of Grendel and Grendel's Mother made by the poet who gave *Beowulf* substantially the form in which it has survived.

4

FICTION AND HISTORY: THE GEATS AFTER BEOWULF'S DEATH

THE borderland between fiction and history in *Beowulf* is a curious field for speculation. By 'history' here I mean little more than some stories or mentions of persons who lived and of things that happened. The heroic traditions known in England in the seventh and later centuries must have been discontinuous. They were distorted by the arts of storytellers as well as by faults of memory. Their subject-matter was not the development or decline of nations, but heroic characters or remarkable events which struck the imagination of poets and held their audiences over several generations. For most people without written records the past closes up behind their grandfathers' time.[1] Hence the transmitters of heroic story lacked chronology in any depth, as may be seen in *Widsith*, where Eormanric from the late fourth century is made contemporary with Alboin who ruled two centuries later. In such conditions historical perspective, or a view of the course of history, was unattainable.

This borderland is the more baffling because the distinction between fact and fiction is seldom clear, and because the poet has the art of giving verisimilitude

[1] In *Beowulf* the principal characters are kept within three generations, which is the common span of memory: King Hrethel, his children and grandchildren (among whom Beowulf is placed); the children and grandchildren of King Healfdene; and, in the story of the Swedish wars, King Ongentheow, his sons and grandsons.

to his stories. That the Danes, Geats, Swedes, and Frisians were contemporary peoples of the west Baltic and the North Sea is historically certain. Hygelac's disastrous raid (c. 525) on the country about the mouth of the Rhine is recorded by a serious historian, Gregory of Tours, within living memory of the event. There is a sufficient probability that Hrothgar and Hrothulf were kings of the Danes, and that Ohthere, Onela, and Eadgils were Swedish kings. But the poem itself is the only evidence that there was a Geatish hero called Beowulf (who is not mentioned in *Widsith* or Scandinavian tradition), that he became king, that he was a contemporary of Hygelac and Hrothgar. His actions in the main plot are fiction, and nothing that is told of him is very probably fact.[1]

The fiction touches the historical background seldom and vaguely. We have seen how the poet got over the difficulty that Hrothulf was at Heorot when Beowulf visited it: throughout over 1,500 lines which describe the visit, neither hero appears to be aware of the other. Vagueness is characteristic of Beowulf's part in the wars between Geats and Swedes, which were very much in the poet's mind and probably have an historical basis. Hs is said to have continued his predecessor's policy of supporting Eadgils against Onela (2392 ff.). In his long reign his initiative appears only in the fight against the Dragon.

[1] That he avenged Hygelac by killing Dæghrefn (2501 ff.) is the one precisely described act that might be historical. But some power of invention should be allowed to a poet, and to make the hero avenge his lord required very little.

What then of Wiglaf, Beowulf's successor? He is given some credentials. He belonged to the family of Wægmundings, of which nothing is known except that Beowulf is also assigned to it. His father was Wihstan, who has been identified on doubtful evidence with the Scandinavian hero Vésteinn,[1] and improbably connected with Wehha, an early East Anglian king. Wiglaf was a 'Swedish prince' (2603), a surprising qualification for Beowulf's nephew, and therefore the less likely to be invented. So there may have been a Scandinavian hero named Wiglaf, though he is unknown to Scandinavian tradition.

On the other hand, everything Wiglaf does in *Beowulf* is fictitious. A poet who knew the story of Sigemund and Fitela (879 ff.) would see the advantages of giving Beowulf a young kinsman, to set the example of heroic devotion in the Dragon Fight, to comfort him when he was mortally wounded, listen to his dying speeches,[2] and lead the Geats when he was dead. There are, of course, disadvantages in introducing a young and attractive hero so near the end of the story. He engages the reader's or listener's interest when it should be fixed on Beowulf, and the poet's way out of the difficulty, though simple, is not altogether satisfying: he says nothing about Wiglaf's future as king of the Geats.

---

[1] Mentioned in *Kálfsvísa* (*Corpus Poeticum Boreale*, i, p. 80), a list of heroes and the horses they rode. The doubt is whether the *Vésteinn* of line 5 is associated with Athils (Eadgils) and Áli (Onela) in lines 7 f.; see E. Björkman, *Studien über die Eigennamen im Beowulf*, Halle, 1920, pp. 118 f.

[2] There are no soliloquies in *Beowulf*.

Many critics suppose that the Geats met with disaster at some time in the sixth century after Hygelac's fall (*c.* 525). Müllenhoff thought that the Geatish kingdom came to an end in the sixth century;[1] Chambers suspected 'that the downfall of the Geatish kingdom and its absorption in Sweden were very possibly brought about by the destruction of Hygelac and all his warriors at the mouth of the Rhine'.[2] In later writers speculation tends to harden into fact. Bonjour writes of 'a defeat [by the Swedes] probably amounting to practical annihilation'.[3] Brodeur also assumes 'the extinction of the Geatish nation'. According to him 'It was Hygelac's death which led to the overthrow of two peoples [Geats and Danes]'.[4]

It is doubtful whether considerations of manpower have much relevance to this tale of marvellous adventures. If they are used, it should be remembered that Hygelac's expedition to the mouth of the Rhine was a ship-borne plundering raid, not one that risked all the men of his nation. Hygelac and a number of picked warriors were lost, but under good rule, recovery should be rapid.[5] That the Geats failed to recover from Hygelac's disaster is not the story of *Beowulf*.

Outside *Beowulf* evidence for the very early history of the Geats is scarce. As far as is known the legends of

---

[1] *Beowulf*, p. 22.　　　　　　　　　[2] *Introduction*[3], p. 13, cf. p. 394.
[3] *The Digressions in 'Beowulf'*, p. 42.
[4] *The Art of 'Beowulf'*, pp. 87, 79.
[5] At least a generation after Hygelac's death, Procopius (*De Bello Gotthico*, ii, 15) noted that the Geats had their own king, and characterized the nation as populous (πολυάνθρωπον); but his information may not have been up to date.

the Teutonic heroic age did not deal with persons and events later than the sixth century. From that time historians depend on Christian sources; but because Christianity came very late to Sweden and Geatland, there is a long gap between the sixth century and Christian references to historical events in these countries. In the account of Europe prefixed to the Old English version of Orosius, the Geats are not mentioned, probably because they were not a strong independent nation at the end of the ninth century. But when or how they lost status between Hygelac's time and King Alfred's is not known from sources outside *Beowulf*.

There is no evidence anywhere for the virtual annihilation of the Geats by the Swedes and much against it. It is unlikely that a people who were wiped out in the sixth century would give their name to a large area of modern Sweden (Västergötland, Östergötland, Götarike), or a title to the reigning Swedish king (*Sveriges, Götes och Vendes Konung*). Icelandic traditions treat the Geats as a distinct people. Harold Fairhair in the early tenth century is credibly reported to have fought many battles against them, and to have won the part of their territory, now Swedish, north of the river Götaelv. For present purposes it is enough to show that they were a distinct and important people at the very end of the Anglo-Saxon period. The Canterbury monk Ailnoth migrated to Odense in Denmark, and there wrote the life of the local martyr King Knud (d. 1086). Beginning with an account of Christianity in Scandinavia about the year 1100, he names five peoples—

Danes, Swedes, Geats, Norwegians, and Icelanders. The Danes, he says, are good Christians; the Norwegians and Icelanders are Christians but, in their hard conditions, do not keep the fasts prescribed by the Church. The Swedes and Geats seem to accept Christianity when times are prosperous, but when adversity comes they persecute Christians and try to drive out Christianity.[1]

The Geats may have been finally subjugated to the loose rule of the Swedish king in the sixth century; but the belief that they were depends on *Beowulf* alone. Is the evidence sure? It derives from two passages—the Geatish woman's[2] lament at Beowulf's funeral (3150–5) and the reference to Geatish women being carried into captivity (3018 ff.) in the Messenger's speech foreboding war when Beowulf's death became known to old enemies. The woman's lament is not a prediction, but an expression of fears natural enough when a great

---

[1] 'Suethi uero et Gothi rebus ad uotum *fl*uentibus prosperisque succedentibus christianitatis fidem nomine tenus uenerari uidentur; at ubi adversitatis aura, siue terrę infertilitate aerisue siccitate aut procellarum densitate, seu hostium incursione uel ignis adustione, inflauerit, fidei religionem, quam uerbo tenus uenerari uidebantur, non modo uerbis uerum rebus christianorumque fidelium persecutionibus insecuntur aque suis finibus omnino expellere conantur' (*Vitae Sanctorum Danorum*, ed. M. Cl. Gertz, Copenhagen, 1908–12, p. 83. I am indebted to the late Paul Grosjean, Bollandist, for a transcript from Gertz's careful text).

[2] Professor Pope's reading *Geatisc meowle* would deserve to be accepted if it were pure conjecture. I take it to mean a typical Geatish woman, like *Afrisc (Ebrisc) meowle* in *Exodus* 580. That the woman was Hygd, Hygelac's widow, and that she had married Beowulf seem very improbable. There is no hint of it in Beowulf's dying speeches; and the woman's lament strikes me as formal, almost perfunctory. The hero's greatness would not be enhanced by a barren political marriage.

protector of his people has died suddenly: war fell hardly on the women of the Heroic Age, and the poet elsewhere emphasizes their sufferings and their interest in peace. The Messenger clearly predicts war; but his reference to the carrying off of Geatish women to a foreign land (3016 ff.) is insufficient to establish the final conquest of the Geats. Wars in those days were not fought out between organized national armies within a limited period. They were more in the nature of raid and counter-raid; and the women in any place that was overrun were part of the plunder. For an Anglo-Saxon poet trained in the heroic tradition, carrying off the women was a concomitant of war, almost like the commonplace raven and wolf which the Messenger refers to in the same passage. So in the battle described in Genesis xiv, the expansion of *Genesis A* 1969 ff. is due to the poet:

> Sceolde forht monig
> blachleor ides   bifiende gan
> on fremdes fæðm.

A successful raid might be followed by a sudden reversal, as in the Bible story. Ongentheow rescued his queen from the Geats (2930). The Swedes were not conquered by the defeat of Ongentheow that followed.

Then, *Beowulf* does not provide clear evidence for the subjugation of the Geats by the Swedes; and it gives some contrary indications. Beowulf's dying speeches, in which prescience might be expected, show no anxiety about the future of his people. If the poet

and his audience knew that the Geats had been conquered by the Swedes near the end of the Heroic Age,
the Messenger would hardly begin with fears of the
Franks and Frisians (2910 ff.), though that is consistent
with an expectation of attacks from one or other old
enemy. And there is still the problem of Wiglaf. If his
reign was disastrous for his people, why was he given
not only the qualities of an heroic leader, but also
extraordinary claims on the goodwill of the Swedes?
He was a 'Swedish prince'; in the Swedish civil wars
the Geats had supported Eadgils who defeated and
killed Onela; and in case Onela's party came back to
power, Wiglaf's father Wihstan had done Onela outstanding service by killing Eanmund, the brother and
ally of Eadgils. To assume that the audience knew
another story about Wiglaf in which all these problems
were unravelled is an easy way out of difficulties.
There is an alternative: that the poet invented what he
thought best for the story he was telling, and did not
trouble about the resulting problems for a kind of
criticism which he could not anticipate.

After all, *Beowulf* is a tale of marvels set in the Heroic
Age—poetic fiction, not history. In the last part the
outcrop of history, or legend based on history, is
obtrusively large; but it need not be extended by
interpretation. The forebodings of war are best taken
as part of the poetic representation of a people's grief
and fears when their great king dies. I have noted
earlier[1] how much the narrative is coloured by the

[1] Above, p. 46.

mood the poet wished to convey. Here his theme is 'King Beowulf is dead'. Had there been occasion to go on to 'Long live King Wiglaf', we might expect to hear of the confident hopes of the Geats for their future under so promising a leader.

IV

CONCLUSION

THE way I have chosen may appear to be one for pedestrian critics. I have supposed that the matters to which the poet gave most space or emphasis are those which he thought it most important to convey; that this kind of poetry depended on expression, not on silences, dark hints or subtle irony. I have preferred the plain meaning of the text because it is present in the mind of any attentive listener or reader who understands the language. Some of the words and some of the names carried associations for Anglo-Saxons that are now lost. But they would vary from person to person; they can seldom be guessed at with a fair chance of being right; and it is questionable whether they are necessary for the enjoyment of *Beowulf*, where so much is explicit. This approach does not imply hostility to conjectural interpretations which aim at giving a deeper meaning to particular passages or to the whole poem. In good hands they have the same exploratory values as other kinds of conjecture. Still, they are an unsafe foundation to build high on; and they are a channel for importing into the poem ideas that may never have occurred to the Anglo-Saxon poet or his audience.

On the audience Professor Whitelock has provided

an admirable short study. I accept her view that they were primarily laymen. Granted that an Anglo-Saxon bishop or priest or monk, or a peasant or a child might enjoy *Beowulf*, there is no sign that it was designed for the special interests which any of these categories brings to mind.

Too little is known about the daily life of laymen in the Anglo-Saxon period, and especially about the entertainments available for their leisure, which must have been the more keenly enjoyed because they were so few. Archaeology has not much to tell about recreations. The ornaments of manuscripts, a rich source in the later Middle Ages, give little help. The early laws and charters do not deal with amusements. Apart from the small remains of secular verse, nearly all the written sources of information come from ecclesiastical circles and are concerned with Church interests. The Church did not encourage sports, games, or entertainments. Early references are mostly warnings to the clergy not to indulge in the pleasures of laymen because they tended to vice, or were unchristian or undignified or unprofitable ways of spending time. One alternative recommended to the clergy—the reading of religious books[1]—could not be recommended to

[1] In a collection of canons (*c.* 1000) attributed to Archbishop Wulfstan, priests are enjoined not to be hunters or hawkers or players of board-games, but to find recreation in their books: *ac plege on his bocum* (ed. K. Jost, *Die 'Institutes of Polity'*, Berne, 1959, p. 202). The one specific literary reference to heroic poetry in early England is Alcuin's, above, p. 49 n. Bede, telling the miracle of Caedmon's inspiration, mentions that the lay workmen of Whitby Abbey, when they took their dinner together, passed the harp round so that each in turn should sing or

English laymen because they were generally illiterate.[1]
Few could read English and fewer could read Latin,
which was the language of nearly all books available
in England before King Alfred's time. It follows that
any book-learning reached them, directly or indirectly,
from the clergy and by word of mouth. That suits well
with the simple and popular references to Scripture
in *Beowulf*—the only references to books that can be
established with certainty.

There remains the question whether the poet himself
was a layman or an ecclesiastic, which is the more
difficult because some who had been educated for the
Church returned to secular life, and because the acti-
vities and interests of men were not always typical of
their class or rank.[2] Whether so influential a churchman

recite some secular piece; but this was a humble sing-song, probably of
old favourites of no great length. In 679 a council at Rome which dealt
with English affairs decreed that bishops and all others who professed
the religious life should not keep harpers or musical equipment or allow
jests and games in their presence (Haddan and Stubbs, *Councils and
Ecclesiastical Documents*, iii, p. 133). The Council of Clovesho in 747 required bishops to see to it that monasteries were not places of amusement
—of 'poets, harpers, musicians, buffoons' (op. cit., p. 369).

[1] Cf. Professor Whitelock, *The Audience of Beowulf*, pp. 19 ff.

[2] A curious happening in later times and different conditions is a
caution against confident inferences from insufficient evidence. Saxo
Grammaticus, reporting the battle of Öland between the Danes and
Estonian pirates in his own day (1170), notes that Lucas, an Englishman
employed as a scribe by the Danish prince Christopher, rallied the
disheartened Danes by recalling former brave deeds. He had very little
book-learning, but an extraordinary knowledge of old stories: 'Tunc
Lucas, Christofori scriba, nacionis Britannice, literis quidem tenuiter
instructus, sed historiarum sciencia apprime eruditus, cum infractos
exercitus nostri animos uideret, mestum ac lugubre silencium clara
uoce prorumpens, sollicitudinem alacritate mutauit. Siquidem memo-
ratis ueterum uirtutibus, nostros ad exigendam a sociorum interfectoribus

as Alcuin was a monk is disputed: he was certainly not a priest; throughout his correspondence he calls himself a deacon—*diaconus, humilis levita*. John the Scot, one of the greatest and most original of Western scholars in the ninth century, seems to have been a layman, *nullis ecclesiasticae dignitatis gradibus insignitus*. Some in all ranks of the clergy had the tastes of laymen; and many laymen who were not very religious were interested in Bible story, lives of saints, and sermons. Critics who describe the poet as an ecclesiastic or, less cautiously, a monk, probably mean that he was literate —that he could read Latin intelligently and perhaps write, attainments seldom to be found except among ecclesiastics. Yet there is no good evidence that the poet could read Latin or write English. Even if the work was written down as parts of it were composed, or immediately after it was completed, dictation was a common practice in those times.[1] And probably all critics would agree that whoever gave us *Beowulf* was expert in the art of composing vernacular heroic poetry, a qualification not to be expected in a typical member of the ordinary clergy or a monastic order.

A well-read continental ecclesiastic wrote *Waltharius*[2]

ulcionem tanta disserendi pericia concitauit, ut non solum mesticiam discuteret, uerum eciam cunctorum pectoribus fortitudinem ingeneraret, dictuque incredibile fuerit, quantum uirium in nostrorum animos ab alienigene hominis sermone manauerit' (ed. Holder, p. 583). If it were not express, who would suppose that Lucas was an Englishman, or that he was by profession a 'scribe', or that, being a scribe, he would have 'small Latin'?

[1] See p. 67 below.
[2] Ed. K. Strecker, *Mon. Germ. Hist. Epist.* vi, 1951, pp. 1 ff. Strecker

(the hero is the Waldere of the Anglo-Saxon fragments), the only example of a Teutonic heroic story that is told at length in Latin verse. The parallel with *Beowulf* is not close, because the Latin medium encourages and exposes a tissue of verbal imitations of favourite poets like Virgil. Yet it has some interest. The poet feels no anachronism in making Walter pray to God, and does not attempt to give the story a Christian turn: his theme is 'the marvellous deeds of a young warrior, not the goodness of God'. But the circle to which it belongs is made clear not only by the chosen medium, but by the first line:

> Tertia pars orbis, fratres, Europa vocatur;

and the last:

> Haec est Waltharii poesis. Vos salvet Iesus.

There is nothing similar in *Beowulf*. Notable, too, is the contrast between the loosely jointed narrative of *Beowulf* and the tidy, orderly way in which the *Waltharius* story is told. Its author has learned from his reading of the *Aeneid* and *Thebaid*. The radical difference from Latin models in the form of *Beowulf*, even more than its style and choice of poetic embroideries, weighs against the view that the author was a member of the clergy well read in Latin.

Some standard of comparison is implied in any

and other modern critics assign *Waltharius* to the later ninth century. The dedicatory prologue by an unidentified 'Geraldus' is printed at vol. v, p. 407 of the same series. There is a doubt whether it is by the author of the poem.

criticism of the structure of *Beowulf*; and there is inconsistency in an attempt to relate its style and content to the tastes of the Anglo-Saxon poet and his audience without inquiring into their feeling for literary form. The difficulty is that no comparable poem survives in Anglo-Saxon or other early Teutonic languages. The longer religious poems are certainly or possibly the work of authors who read Latin and might be influenced by Latin standards. In their construction some, notably *Elene* and *Andreas*, follow a Latin source closely enough to retain its orderly shape. But a remarkably high proportion of those that treat their subjects freely raise problems of construction. *Genesis* has a clearly defined interpolation from an Old Saxon original, poetically valuable but disproportioned in the whole poem. The extant text of *Exodus* has been explained by mechanical displacement or interpolation. The long Azarias passage breaks the flow in *Daniel*. The question whether the verses grouped under the modern title *Christ and Satan* were intended to make one poem is open. The unity of *Christ* has been often debated. Good critics have taken some thirty lines which follow it in the Exeter Book to be the beginning of *Guthlac A* as the manuscript indicates, or the end of *Christ*, or a fragment unconnected with either. There are differences of opinion about the relation of *Fates of the Apostles* to *Andreas*. However these irregularities and ambiguities are explained, they suggest that a keen sense of literary form, which seems to have come naturally to the best Greek authors and is characteristic of the French in later times, was not widespread among the Anglo-Saxons.

It would be unreasonable to apply to *Beowulf* classical standards which the audience and probably the poet could not know. But on any reasonable standards (and without any, discussion is unhelpful) it is architecturally inferior to the *Odyssey*, or the *Chanson de Roland*, or *Sir Gawain and the Green Knight*. It has enough high qualities without the claim to structural elegance.

NOTE A

THE TRANSMISSION OF *BEOWULF*

Two main possibilities may be distinguished: (i) That the poem was written down by the poet, or at his dictation, before it was made known to readers or listeners, and thereafter was transmitted in writing. Modern conditions give a bias in favour of this view, since all who study *Beowulf* are concerned with books and writing. It fosters confidence in the one late manuscript as a reproduction of the original, and encourages the kind of mechanical textual criticism which depends on the confusion of one letter with another in the course of copying. (ii) That the poem was composed without writing, and recited from memory by trained entertainers until it was recorded, perhaps at the request of a king or noble who heard and admired it, and wanted to be sure that he could hear it again in private or in company. This second view seems to me the more probable. It adds greatly to the difficulties of textual criticism; for the text would be more liable to change when it depended on the memory and choice of successive reciters: the poet himself might vary it from one recitation to another.

Whichever alternative is preferred, it is likely that the text was first written down with a stylus (*græf*) on wax tablets (*weaxbrædu*), the usual material for drafts throughout Anglo-Saxon times.[1] Henry Bradley suggested that it was first written on irregular pieces of parchment (or vellum),

---

[1] On the medieval use of wax tablets see W. Wattenbach, *Das Schriftwesen im Mittelalter*, 4th ed., Graz, 1958, pp. 63 ff.

and that for other long poems regular sheets of four pages were used.[1] But wax was cheap and parchment dear. Wax could easily be corrected, whereas erasure on parchment needs time and care. And writing on wax tablets could be preserved long enough to permit considered revision. After revision the tablets would be transcribed into the normal quires that make a codex. If tablets were used for the first recording, a calligraphic script from the beginning of the written tradition cannot be assumed. Nor can scholarly checking of copies be relied on. It is surprising how few corrections of obvious faults are found in the surviving poetical manuscripts.

Evidence for beginning the more conservative written tradition a good while before the extant manuscript (*c.* 1000) comes from the high technical quality of the verse; the preservation, irregular but well scattered, of forms that can be reasonably established by the metre and that are early rather than late;[2] and the avoidance of some syntactical usages that are common in a comparable late work such as *Maldon*. How late could such a text be preserved, or even reshaped, without the help of writing? Popular memory may be ruled out as a way of preserving the text of a long poem. Perhaps the best answer is: so long as there was a good *scop* trained in the old tradition. I mean a professional accustomed to entertain an audience by re-telling versified stories of the Heroic Age; not a poet like Cynewulf, who was almost certainly an ecclesiastic, literate above the ordinary; who, as far as is known, confined himself

---

[1] 'The Numbered Sections in O.E. Poetical MSS.', *Proc. Brit. Acad.* vii (delivered 1915), pp. 17 f. of the separate print.

[2] The use of these forms for dating poems is open to many doubts. They could not be decisive proof that the whole poem was an early composition. Archaic forms may be used as proper to the kind of poetry, or for metrical convenience, or in old-established formulas, or in verses remembered from an earlier poem on the same subject.

to paraphrasing Latin religious texts of which there was no previous rendering in Anglo-Saxon verse; and whose signed poems have a written tradition from the outset.

Unfortunately little can be known about the later history of this dignified class of entertainers. But at the very end of the eighth century (797) Alcuin urged upon Higbald of Lindisfarne, a senior bishop of good reputation, that a Christian lector should be heard in the refectory, not a minstrel (*citharista*) telling the heathen story of Ingeld. It cannot reasonably be supposed that such entertainers disappeared immediately afterwards from the households of great laymen, or that the author of *Brunanburh* (937) learned his correct verse and warlike diction entirely from texts that had been preserved in writing for well over a century. The limits of time within which *Beowulf* might have been committed to writing are wide.

Nor can much be learned from MS. Vitellius A xv about the length or age of the chain of manuscripts that preceded it. Elsewhere I have noted some evidence that the *Letter of Alexander to Aristotle* and *Beowulf* were transcribed from the same manuscript;[1] and a number of errors in the extant text are rightly explained by careless copying. Probably there were several written predecessors, but more than one cannot be proved. We can, however, be sure that Vitellius A xv was not directly copied from a much older manuscript which turned up towards the end of the tenth century. The first scribe of *Beowulf* copied also three prose pieces, each of which has its own linguistic peculiarities;[2] so that generally his copying was mechanical, and must have followed exemplars, for the prose and for *Beowulf*, which were considerably influenced by Late West Saxon usage.

A succession of manuscripts would account for the fairly even modernization of linguistic forms throughout *Beowulf*.

[1] *Studies*, &c., p. 94.   [2] Ibid., pp. 88 ff.

On the deeper changes that might result from many copyings, there is a lack of direct evidence. No part of *Beowulf* or of the other remains of heroic narrative (*Waldere* fragments, *Finnsburh* fragment) survives in a second manuscript. But in other kinds, mostly religious, there are places where two sources for the text overlap, notably in the fragment *Azarias* which appears in the Exeter Book and also in MS. Junius 11 (*Daniel* 279 ff.).[1] In these double recordings there are substantial variations, more extensive than would be expected in Anglo-Saxon copies of a Latin text like Virgil or Prudentius. When they were copying their own language, some at least in the succession of writers did more than make mechanical errors. Modernization was a natural tendency. Possibilities of expansion or omission occurred to transmitters. Sometimes other half-lines that served well enough in the context, or other words that passed in the alliteration, floated into their minds as they wrote or dictated. So there is a looseness of transmission, common enough in Middle English, rather than reproduction with ritual accuracy.

In its manuscript transmission *Beowulf* is not likely to have been exempt from such variations. To say that 'no other poet in Anglo-Saxon England composed poetry comparable with *Beowulf*'[2] is to assert what cannot be

---

[1] For a survey of these passages see K. Sisam, *Studies*, &c., pp. 31 ff. As additional examples, note:

Azarias 14	nu we þec for þearfum	ond for þreanydum:
Daniel 293	nu we þec for þreaum	and for ðeonydum
Azarias 74	woruldsceafta wuldor	ond weorca gehuylc:
Daniel 363	woruldcræfta wlite	and weorca gehwilc.

[2] Brodeur, *The Art of 'Beowulf'*, p. 2. That *Beowulf* is the only long heroic poem to survive from the Anglo-Saxon period is not really evidence of its superiority to all other poetry known at that time. Of course, survival depended on somebody valuing it who was influential enough to secure the making of the first manuscript; and on others who had subsequent copies made. If, as seems probable, the manuscripts were made by

known. But if it were true, there is no evidence that Anglo-Saxons recognized it in a way that would secure special respect for the text: for example, by choosing the poem for recital on official occasions, as the Athenians chose the *Iliad* and the *Odyssey*. Whether in an oral or a written transmission, changes are to be expected which methodical textual criticism cannot detect, because its resources are so slight in this case.

With so many uncertainties, a textual critic has no simple prescription for improving the text. Complete scepticism is a barren doctrine. Undisciplined guessing cannot be justified, though conjectures that are not in themselves acceptable may be valuable in exposing a difficulty or opening the way to a solution. The ultra-conservatism which has predominated for many years in this branch of Anglo-Saxon studies has serious weaknesses: apart from its tendency towards dullness, it leads to neglect of intelligent conjecture, and encourages over-straining of sense, grammar, or metre in the defence of the transmitted text. To make the best of the one late manuscript requires judgement, a sense of style, and interest in anything that throws light on Anglo-Saxon feeling, thought, or expression.

scribes employed in the scriptoria of churches, the elevated tone of the poem would be in its favour. The Christian colouring might help, though it was not essential: there is nothing Christian in either of the two tracts—*Wonders of the East* and *Alexander's Letter to Aristotle*—which the first hand of the extant manuscript copied immediately before *Beowulf*, and there is a good deal that is obtrusively heathen in the second of these. But the survival of any old manuscript in Anglo-Saxon would depend more on chance than on literary quality. From the twelfth century to the time of antiquarian collectors in the sixteenth, *Beowulf* was unintelligible; and if the contents of the codex rather than blind chance were a condition of survival in that period, the rude coloured illustrations to *Wonders of the East* were more likely to save it.

NOTE B

CHRISTIANITY IN *BEOWULF*

THAT *Beowulf*, as we have it, comes from a christianized community is certain; but scholars of the first rank differ on the question how deeply Christianity enters into its structure. Klaeber, we have seen,[1] believed that the hero in some way symbolized Christ. I note three other opinions, each the result of a careful discussion that should be read complete.

Chadwick argued 'that the great bulk of the poem must have been in existence—not merely as a collection of lays or stories, but in full epic form—an appreciable time before the middle of the seventh century'.[2] He supposed that a pagan epic was adapted to the feeling of a Christian audience, and that the elementary character of the Christian references points to a minstrel who perhaps drew most of his knowledge from Christian poems in English. Professor Tolkien, who assigns the poem to the age of Bede (d. 737), thinks that the Christian poet represented Beowulf as a noble pagan.[3] Professor Whitelock concludes that the audience for whom *Beowulf* was composed was 'steeped in Christian doctrines'.[4] For this and other reasons she considers any time in the eighth century as a possible date for the poem.[5]

At any time to which the composition can be reasonably assigned, moderately informed Anglo-Saxons would know from traders, missionaries, and other travellers across the

---

[1] Above, pp. 19 f.   [2] *The Heroic Age*, p. 56.   [3] *Beowulf*, &c., pp. 42 ff.
[4] *The Audience of 'Beowulf'*, p. 21.   [5] Op. cit., p. 29.

North Sea that the Danes, Geats, and Swedes had been in earlier times and were still heathen. So the narrative itself, which concerns these peoples, involved no conflict between Christians and heathens of the kind that is implicit in *Maldon* and express throughout the *Chanson de Roland*. Besides, it was necessary that, in the conflicts with monsters, Beowulf, Hrothgar, Wiglaf, and others on the right side should have the sympathy of an audience who belonged to a christianized community: sympathy would be lost if the heathen character of the heroes was emphasized. Let us see how the poet handles this delicate problem.

(i) For him the word *hæðen* has always an evil connotation. It is used only once of men, in the much debated passage where Hrothgar's people turn to idols for help;[1] it is twice applied to their enemy Grendel (852, 986).

(ii) There are few references to distinctively heathen practices. The Church condemned *augurias vel divinationes*,[2] and before Beowulf set out on his voyage to Heorot, the Geats *hæl sceawedon* (204), which may be rendered 'took the omens'. There is no adverse comment from the poet; and perhaps the meaning in this context is simply that they observed the natural signs of a favourable wind and sea.

Cremation, not burial, is the accepted practice—at Hnæf's funeral, where the description is vivid,[3] and at

---

[1] I see nothing in this passage (175 ff.) to establish the view that any part of it has been added to a text essentially the same as that which has come down to us. There is inconsistency in making Hrothgar's people turn to idols; but the poem has many inconsistencies, and probably the audience did not notice them. As I understand the poet, he is emphasizing here the desperate state of the Danes before Beowulf came to deliver them: they had tried in vain every remedy they could think of. He might have made them pray to God, so that Beowulf's coming would be the answer to their prayer, but he does not choose that way.

[2] e.g. Egbert's *Penitential*, c. 750, in Haddan and Stubbs, *Councils and Ecclesiastical Documents*, iii, p. 420.

[3] For how long would a striking event be remembered, not as a vague

Beowulf's. It is implied in the regret that Æschere's body could not be burnt because Grendel's mother had devoured it (2124 ff.). Cremation, never general in Anglo-Saxon England, seems to have been dying out in heathen times, and to have been obsolete by the end of the seventh century when the last pagan courts were converted. Burial was the only Christian practice, yet the poet makes no adverse comment on cremation. The probable explanation is that the dying or obsolete custom was felt to be a negligible danger to Christianity in England. As the traditional rite in heroic poetry, it would not offend Anglo-Saxon Christians.[1]

But when Hrothgar's people turned to their idols for help (175 ff.) an emphatic comment makes clear the folly and wickedness of idol-worship. The explanation is, I suggest, that idol-worship was felt to be a present danger to Christianity. There is evidence for it in England almost up to the end of the eighth century, when the Scandinavian invasions brought a new wave of heathenism. In his *Dialogue* Egbert, archbishop of York (732–66), debars from the priesthood *idola adorantes*; and in his *Penitential* he provides penances for those who make offerings, great or small, to demons.[2]

(iii) The poem shows no interest in theological niceties. For example, Grendel, a devil (939, 1680), tried to escape and join the multitude of devils (*secan deofla gedræg* 756).

---

tradition, but in considerable detail, without written record or verse memorial? From observation I should say rather more than 130 years under favourable conditions. The Sutton Hoo ship-burial, or a contemporary cremation, might be remembered at the end of the eighth century. If the event were commemorated in verse and there were professional reciters or storytellers to transmit it, the period could be longer.

[1] There were decrees against cremation in Charlemagne's empire, where it persisted in some German districts. As far as I know, there is no mention of it in the decrees of Anglo-Saxon church councils or in English penitentials, where other heathen practices are censured.

[2] Haddan and Stubbs, iii, pp. 410 and 420.

When he plunged into the mere, mortally wounded, 'Hell received him'. But Beowulf thinks of him as awaiting God's decree on Judgement Day (977 ff.). No attempt is made to explain the apparently different conceptions.

(iv) An audience who had renounced heathenism would be prejudiced against the heroes if they were shown as wor-shippers of Woden or Thunor. Geats and Danes alike— Beowulf and Hygelac, Hrothgar and Wealhtheow—thank God for help or favour (nobody thanks the inexorable Wyrd). But Christ is not mentioned. This simple mono-theism is in keeping with the Scriptural allusions. The Creation (90 ff.), Cain and Abel (106 ff., 1261 ff.), the Flood (1689 ff.), the Judgement (978, 2742, 3069),[1] stick in the minds of children. There are no references to the Gospels; and though it can fairly be said that the story does not call for them, in a form which allows so many comments and digressions they could easily have been introduced.

So far the case seems to be strong for Chadwick's opinion that the stage of Christianity represented in *Beowulf* is elementary. Yet Professor Whitelock reaches the opposite conclusion—'that the audience of *Beowulf* was thoroughly acquainted with the Christian religion';[2] that so far from beginning with the Old Testament or with Genesis (which provides most of the Scriptural allusions) Christian teachers 'preached first of the major doctrines; they spoke of the Redemption of the world by Christ's Passion; the detailed stories of the Old Testament could be left till later'.

I am seldom inclined to differ from Professor Whitelock's

[1] Following Sievers, I take this passage (3069–73) to be an interpolation in the sense that it has been added to a text substantially the same as that which has come down to us; in other words, that it is not the work of the poet as defined at p. 2 above. See *R.E.S.* N.S. ix, 1958, pp. 130 f.

[2] Op. cit., p. 8.

interpretation, but do not find it altogether satisfying in this point. Certainly the primary task of missionaries and priests was to teach the Gospel. Yet Caedmon began with the Creation, not with the Passion: and, according to Bede, he later worked through the Old and the New Testament under his instructors. When wise Bishop Daniel advised Boniface how to convince heathens by argument, he suggested subjects more akin to Genesis than to the Gospels.[1] In weighing the Christian element in *Beowulf*, we have to consider what laymen with a not very distant heathen background would readily absorb and remember; and Genesis was in the forefront of Christian teaching to laymen, partly because it was the beginning of the whole Biblical narrative, perhaps more because most men were interested in such problems as the origin of the world, of mankind, of the supernatural beings in whom they believed. On these problems many pagan races have speculated, often crudely. In the early chapters of Genesis, Christian teachers had answers that were simple, coherent, and of the highest poetical quality.

Still, an elementary stage of Christianity is compatible with Miss Whitelock's comparatively late range for the date of composition. If there were no other evidence than the Christian allusions, one could safely infer that *Beowulf* was earlier than the post-Conquest *Chanson de Roland*, where the heroes have benediction and absolution, and saints carry them to Paradise; or than the thirteenth-century *Nibelungenlied*, where the motives of the plot are savage, but Christian forms are a matter of course: Siegfried has a cathedral funeral, Gunther takes a chaplain with him on his journey, and, if tradition forbade making Attila a Christian, he practises religious tolerance, and mass may be celebrated

[1] Mon. Germ. Hist., *Epist. Merovingici et Karolini Aevi*, i, p. 271.

at his court. These heroic poems belong to a later period of Western Christianity. But in England, where even nominal Christianity was not established in all kingdoms until the late seventh century,[1] one would expect at that time, or in the eighth, or even the early ninth century, a gradation from near-paganism to the Christianity of Cuthbert, Bede, or Alcuin. The Christian allusions in *Beowulf* are of the kind that would be readily appreciated by the audience I have assumed,[2] i.e. all the company assembled for entertainment in the hall of a great layman, among whom there would be more and less instructed, more and less devout.

Of course the poet knew much more of the Scriptures than he put into *Beowulf*, whether he learned it from preachers or from Christian poetry in the vernacular or from books. But how deep was his Christianity on the evidence of the text? Professor Tolkien supposed that he represented the Heroic Age to a Christian audience as pagan, noble, and hopeless, and that the hero himself is shown as essentially pagan. If by 'Christian' is meant one who accepts the teaching of the Gospels, then Beowulf is a noble pagan, whether or not his references to God, God's light, and Judgement can be explained away. But great difficulties stand in the way of all explanations that make the poet a deep thinker, attempting themes and ways of conveying them that might be tried on a select body of readers in a more advanced age. Hrothgar does not fit into the picture of a pagan age. 'He refers all things to the favour of God, and

---

[1] According to Felix of Crowland, who knew him personally, Cissa, Guthlac's successor in the hermitage there, was still unbaptized among heathens, presumably English, in the early years of the eighth century (ed. B. Colgrave, 1956, ch. 148). Nobody who has lived among an intelligent people in the early generations of missionary work could suppose that, when a king and his immediate supporters were converted, all his people became informed in Christian doctrine.

[2] Above, pp. 8 ff.

never omits thanks for mercies.'[1] He does not express an unchristian thought. He is represented as noble but certainly not pagan.

I prefer a simpler explanation: that in this work the poet was not much concerned with Christianity and paganism. Beowulf was a hero mainly because of his deeds. All his adventures come from pagan stories, and the pagan motives and actions persist. Hrothgar is made eminent by his speeches, which were not governed by pagan tradition. The Christian poet was free to mould them as he wished, and so to make belief in God a leading feature of the character. He was likely to make the most of it, since Hrothgar is not just the pathetic figure of a king incapable through old age of protecting his people: he is a famous hero, still great because of his wisdom and goodness.

The same hand drew both characters and both are intended to be admired. There is no criticism of anything Beowulf says or does, however unchristian it may be. His doctrine of revenge, his eagerness for material rewards and earthly fame, his silence about a future life, all pass without comment. His satisfaction that God cannot blame him for the murder of kinsmen (2741 f.) is paralleled in the poet's earlier praise: 'he did not slay his comrades in their cups' (2179 f.). And it is worth noting that, if all Hrothgar's speeches are accepted as belonging to the original composition, they put forward no characteristically Christian doctrine. Most intelligent men would agree that overweening is a vice, especially in the crude forms that Hrothgar thinks of—miserliness, rapacity, and the wanton killing of companions (1709 ff.). Reversals of fortune (1769 ff.) are a commonplace subject of reflection and story among pagans. So are the shortness and uncertainty

---

[1] Tolkien, *Beowulf*, &c., p. 43.

of human life (1753 ff.): Homer had said more concisely that ten thousand ways of death lie close about us, and no man can flee or avoid them.

In short, there is little in *Beowulf* that is distinctively Christian in the strict sense. The words and conduct of the ideal characters are for the most part designed to show qualities such as courage, loyalty, generosity, and wisdom, which are admired by good men of any creed. Other characteristics, such as determination to exact vengeance, are not in accord with Christian doctrine, but were probably still admired by the majority of Anglo-Saxons in Christian times.

NOTE C

HROTHGAR AND HROTHULF

1164   *þa gyt wæs hiera sib ætgædere*

(i) What seems to be implied is a final breach between Hrothgar and Hrothulf. The implication cannot be extended to a quarrel that arose after Hrothgar's death.

(ii) The words in themselves do not imply treachery on Hrothulf's part, any more than on Hrothgar's.

(iii) Two other passages are used to support the view that the friendly association ended in violent dissension.

(*a*) *Widsith* 45 ff.

> Hroþwulf ond Hroðgar   heoldon lengest
> sibbe ætsomne   suhtorfædran
> siþþan hy forwræcon   Wicinga cynn
> ond Ingeldes   ord forbigdan
> forheowan æt Heorote   Heaðobeardna þrym.

The likeness of the second line to *Beowulf* 1164 can hardly be accidental. Beowulf and Hygelac have no place in Widsith's catalogue; and the longer poem, which makes so much use of the Scylding background, is unlikely to have borrowed from *Widsith* only this one line. Both probably echo a traditional verse in which *sib* and *suhter(ge)fæderan* made the alliteration: for metrical reasons *ætsomne* is preferred in a first, *ætgædere* in a second half-line. But, taken by themselves, these lines do not suggest a final quarrel between Hrothgar and Hrothulf. There was a natural limit to their

alliance, which must end when one or the other died. From
the similar use of *lengest* in *Widsith* 28

> Sigehere lengest   Sæ-Denum weold

we do not infer that Sigehere was deposed or assassinated.

(*b*) *Beowulf* 1015 ff.

>   magas wæran
> swiðhicgende   on sele þam hean,
> Hroðgar ond Hroþulf.   Heorot innan wæs
> freondum afylled,   nalles facenstafas
> Þeod-Scyldingas   þenden fremedon.

This is from the account of the feast in Heorot after Beowulf's
victory over Grendel.

To translate *facenstafas* (found only here) by 'treachery'
prejudices the discussion. *Facen* means any kind of wickedness,
and *facenstafas* 'wrongful acts (against the community)'. It
would cover, e.g., acts of cowardice, disobedience, false
swearing, as well as treachery. *Nalles* is sometimes used to
begin a negative variation of a preceding positive state-
ment; in the simplest form, 3019 *oft, nalles æne* 'often, not
once only'; or, with a clause,

1749 f.

> gytsað gromhydig,   nallas on gylp seleð
> fætte beagas.

So far the natural meaning is that all the company were
good and united. The implication of trouble ahead depends
on interpreting *þenden* 'at that time' in the light of two
assumptions: that *þenden* is contrasted with a particular
time of dissension among the Danes which this vague state-
ment brought to the minds of the audience; and that it
could only be the time of a final quarrel between Hrothgar
and Hrothulf.

An interpretation so deeply rooted in modern criticism

may seem to be beyond question now. Yet it depends very little on what is known, and very much on assumptions or conjectures, or on favourable inclination where there is a reasonable doubt. The poet's comment at the end of the scene in Heorot might be expected to give its keynote. There (1246 ff.) he says unequivocally that the Danes were warlike, disciplined, and good subjects: the last words are *wæs seo þeod tilu*: 'that was a good people.' A few lines earlier (1228 ff.) Wealhtheow praises the company for the same good qualities. The whole scene describes the splendour of life in Heorot, and serves to rehabilitate the Danes, who had been in an unfavourable light while they had no answer to Grendel's raids and their champions could be taunted with lack of courage (590 ff.). The same purpose of rehabilitation appears when we are told that Hrothgar and Hrothulf were sure Unferth was a brave man, although they knew his faults (1166 ff.). So in line 1019 *þenden* 'at that time' could mean 'in the age of heroes' or 'in the great days of Heorot', with the simple connotation that those glorious times were past.

Everything hangs on the meaning of *þa gyt wæs hiera sib ætgædere*. It can be explained as an allusion to a final breach between Hrothgar and Hrothulf. Yet nothing is known of such a quarrel: that it was about the succession is a guess, not to be found in medieval sources. And there is a possible alternative. Suppose that, as the *Widsith* reference suggests, the names of Hrothgar and Hrothulf called to mind a long harmonious co-operation, strong enough to break Ingeld's attack on Heorot, rather than its dissolution. Then the clause could mean 'the good pair of kinsmen were still together (*when Beowulf visited Heorot*)'. This supposition may seem relatively uninteresting; but it has the advantage of dispensing with a story built up in modern times on very slight foundations.

NOTE D

THRYTH

UNCRITICAL use has been made of the thirteenth-century *Vitae Duorum Offarum* from St. Albans (ed. Chambers, *Introduction*[3], pp. 217 ff.). According to this romance the Continental Offa (Offa I) rescued an unnamed daughter of the King of York in distress and married her. In his absence, by means of a forged letter, this innocent woman was cast away in a desolate place and her children were murdered. Then by the intervention of a good hermit all ended happily. His descendant, the Mercian Offa (Offa II), married a kinswoman of Charlemagne who had arrived in England after being set adrift in a boat for a terrible crime. So her name 'Drida' became 'Quendrida, id est regina Drida' (representing OE. *Cwenðryð*). To Offa's great sorrow she contrived the murder of St. Ethelbert; and she came to a miserable end.

Neither story resembles the *Beowulf* episode. But by discarding the legend of Offa I and substituting part of the legend of Offa II, Offa I is given a criminal queen called Drida; and although the essentials of the episode are still wanting, the supposed Drida is identified with the supposed Thryth.

The historical wife of Offa II was called Cynethryth, not Cwenthryth, as documents and coins prove; there is no early evidence against her character, and the name continued in favour among good families after her day: St. Dunstan's mother was called Cynethryth. The obvious purpose in the *Vitae* was to clear Offa II of responsibility for the murder of a saint, against earlier authorities like the Chronicle which says bluntly under 792: 'Offa ordered Ethelbert to be beheaded.'

To be closely related to a royal martyr was dangerous for a woman's later reputation. The ninth-century abbess whose name really was Cwenthryth was made the murderer of her brother St. Kenelm; and St. Edward's mother Ælfthryth was saddled with his murder (see Stenton, *Anglo-Saxon England*, p. 368; K. Sisam, *Medium Ævum*, xxii (1953), p. 24). By an odd chance the names of these three women all end in -*thryth*, which was a common second element in feminine names; but plain *Thryth* is not found among Anglo-Saxon proper names.

The reasonable explanation of the *Vitae* is that 'Drida' has its origin in the etymology of Quendrida (*id est regina Drida*), mistakenly supposed to be the name of the queen of Offa II; and that the story of that queen's wickedness is a post-Conquest invention by a writer at the monastery of St. Albans, which claimed Offa II as its founder, and so had a strong motive for clearing his name.

INDEX

Ælfthryth, queen, made murderess of St. Edward in late legend, 84.

Ailnoth, notice of Geats, *c.* 1100, 55 f.

Alcuin: a deacon, 63; reproves heroic story of Ingeld among clergy, 49 n., 61 n., 69.

Alexander's Letter to Aristotle, see *Epistola Alexandri*.

Andreas, relation to *Fates of the Apostles*, 65; form 65.

audience, the: the hall-company, 8 ff.; primarily laymen and unlettered, 60 ff., 72 ff.; their knowledge and degree of attention, 9 n., 10, 60; tastes and interests, 10 ff.; attitude to Heroic Age, 42 f.; feeling for literary form, 13, 65 f.

Azarias, relation of text to *Daniel*, 65.

Beowulf: a unique survival, 27, 65, 70 n.; an heroic narrative, 1; poetic fiction, 58; for entertainment, 16; its length, 2; native development or imitation of classics?, 3, 64; possible methods of composition, 3 n., 67; recitation in instalments?, 4 f.; no forward references, 4 n.; unifying factors in plot, 5 ff.; completeness, 6 f.; dignity, 8, 13 f.; fine language, 10 and n.; verisimilitude, 45 f., 47, 51; diversity of mood and subject-matter, 16, 32, 39, 46 f., 58 f.; Christian element, 19 f., 72 ff.; elegiac

element, 16; the search for ulterior meanings, 26 ff.; Müllenhoff's interpretation, 17 f.; Tolkien's interpretation, 20, 24 ff.; no soliloquies in, 53 n.; no quick dialogue, 38; supposed dramatic irony, 36 n.; textual criticism, 67 ff.; opinions on date, 68 and n., 72, 76 f.; *see* Heroic Age; Poet; *Waltharius*.

Beowulf: the scourge of monsters, 24; never defeated, 25 f.; wholly fictitious?, 52; Hygelac's man and kinsman, 14 f.; refuses Hygd's offer of throne, 37 n.; becomes ideal king, 15; supposed marriage to Hygd, 56 n.; his death, 7; his eagerness for rewards, 20; for booty, 12 n.; for treasure, 11 f., 20; for earthly fame, 20; noble manners, 13 f.; fearless of death, 26; Christian or pagan?, 19 f., 77 f.; contrast with Hrothgar, 22 f.; with Wiglaf, 23 f.; with Heremod, 29 n.; the poet's appreciation, 12 n., 45, 78.

Bjarkamál, 37.

Breca episode, 14, 23, 41.

Brunanburh, metre and diction, 69.

Caedmon: kind of entertainment he avoided, 61 n.; the Creation his first subject, 76.

Chadwick, H. M.: on date, 72; on Christian element, 72, 75.

Chanson de Roland: literary form, 66; conflict of Christian and